CONTENTS

10

26

STEPPING OUT AS A ROYAL

After the engagements had been announced, Diana and Kate undertook their first official duties alongside their fiancées. Both women were now the centre of attention as royal wedding fever began to take hold

Lady Di takes the plunge

TUESDAY, MARCH 10, 1981

64

A Troubled WOMAN

As the 1990s dawned, Diana was increasingly isolated as her marriage to Charles gradually fell apart, and she grew tired of incessant media attention

The rivals

WEDNESDAY, JULY 11, 1991

Diana weeps for her dad

MONDAY, MARCH 28, 1992

The broken spirit

TUESDAY, NOVEMBER 9, 1993

A YOUNG BRIDE
In LOVE

Prince William and Kate Middleton's wedding was a spectacular occasion. The spontaneity of the day demonstrated how the monarchy has changed since Diana, who would have turned 50 on July 1, came into our lives

By Victoria Murphy
Daily Mirror Royal Reporter

Bride Kate Middleton walked out onto the balcony of Buckingham Palace and gasped: "Oh wow".

Standing side-by-side with her new husband Prince William, it was the moment the 29-year-old stepped into life as a member of the royal family.

Her now iconic balcony appearance at 1pm on Friday, April 29, 2011, took place almost exactly 30 years to the day that William's mum, Princess Diana, made her royal debut in her marriage to Prince Charles.

Staring out at the thousands that lined London's Mall, both brides gawped in awe as they saw first-hand the euphoria that their weddings had inspired across the nation.

Both Kate and Diana had been presented with the same dazzling diamond and sapphire engagement ring, and both were destined for stardom the moment they said "I do".

From the day her engagement to William was announced on November 16, 2010, Kate was thrust into the limelight as the dazzling new jewel in the royal family crown.

With her tall, slender frame, trademark dark hair and elegant style, her image adorned the front pages of newspapers and magazines around the world.

For the first time in years the face of royalty could sell anything from calendars to tea towels, dolls to pill boxes. There was no corner of the globe untouched by Kate's star power.

Not since Diana had the world found a royal bride so captivating. And on Kate's wedding day there was only one thing the cheering crowds wanted to see.

"We want Kate. We want Kate", thousands of voices shouted from outside Buckingham Palace, before urging: "Kiss, kiss, kiss" as their chants reached a deafening crescendo.

And the new royal couple did not disappoint. Leaning towards his bride, William said to Kate: "Are you ready? Okay, let's." At 1.27pm

the prince kissed his wife on the lips.

And the crowds whooped with delight when, just three minutes later, he leaned in again, telling Kate: "Let's give them another one. I love you."

Kate must have known that, as she gave her new husband a second kiss at 1.30pm, their 'balcony moment' would be a picture that graced millions of iconic newspaper front pages the next day.

And as the screaming crowds watched from below, no-one could fail to be reminded of the day when 20-year-old Diana became the first royal bride to kiss her husband.

On July 29, 1981, a reluctant Charles said to Di: "They are trying to get us to kiss."

She responded: "Well, how about it?" Their peck became one of the most enduring images in royal history. And Kate and William's image will do the same.

Kate woke up on the morning of her wedding just plain Miss Middleton, the daughter of an air hostess and great-granddaughter of a miner.

By the end of the day she was standing in the palace next to the Queen, a fully-fledged member of the royal family.

At 11am on April 29 she had taken the long, slow walk on the arm of her father Michael, down the aisle of Westminster Abbey, past 1,900 friends, family and official guests.

An audience of two billion people watched on screen, transfixed, as Kate stepped out of the black Rolls Royce Phantom VI in her ivory satin and lace Sarah Burton gown.

The dress that had been shrouded in secrecy for months was finally on display.

Critics would later hail it a fashion triumph, but Kate's only concern had been that her husband-to-be thought she looked great. And, of course, he did.

As she arrived at the altar, William told her: "You look lovely.

All wave: The wedding day was a hugely patriotic occasion

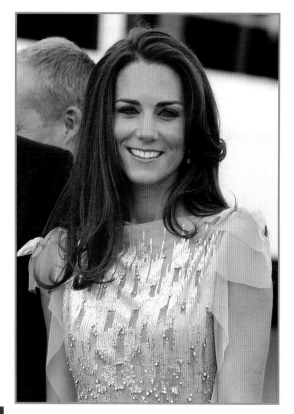

You look beautiful", before they looked into each other's eyes and relayed the vows that made Kate the future Queen.

After months of planning and anticipation their special day went without a hitch, and the Queen herself described it as "amazing".

It may have been a bank holiday and a semi-state occasion, but William and Kate had been determined to make it a day full of unstuffy and intimate moments.

And it was also full of surprises. Crowds squealed with delight when the couple drove through the streets of London in Prince Charles's Aston Martin with JU5T WED on the plates in a scene that millions will recognise from weddings the world over.

The message of the day was clear – we are a new generation of royals. We do things differently.

And as the self-made Middleton family with their working-class roots stood side by side with the blue-blooded royals on the Buckingham Palace balcony, no-one batted an eyelid except to wipe away tears of joy.

A hundred or even 50 years ago the marriage may have been frowned upon. Now it was celebrated as a day when, as father of the bride, Michael Middleton said in his speech, "equality ruled". Kate's walk down the aisle may only have been three minutes long, but her journey to the palace began many years before.

She first met William as a regular 19-year-old living across the hall from him in St Andrews University St Salvator's Hall, and behind the closed doors of student life their friendship grew into love.

The kiss: William and Kate's balcony scenes evoked many memories from 30 years ago

In the years that followed they would live together, study together, go out into the working world together and develop a trusted circle of close-knit friends.

It wasn't always plain sailing. Their relationship hit a notorious rocky patch during the summer of 2007, when they split for a few months before eventually finding their way back into each other's arms.

It took William almost 10 years to finally propose, and the prince later told how he waited until it was the "right time" to make the huge gesture he knew would change his sweetheart's life forever.

He eventually got down on one knee in October 2010, in a remote log cabin on holiday in Kenya.

He said: "I was planning it and then it just felt really right out in Africa. It was beautiful at the time."

It was then William, 28, produced the ring he had been carrying in his rucksack for weeks – the engagement ring that first belonged to Princess Diana.

It was a heartfelt and personal gesture which, he said, was his way of keeping Diana "close to it all" so she didn't miss "all the fun and excitement" of the wedding.

And as he slipped the 18-carat sapphire and diamond rock onto Kate's finger, he brought his fiancée a step closer to following in the footsteps of the woman that became renowned the world over as the "People's Princess".

Since then comparisons between Kate and Diana have been impossible for the new royal to avoid.

Their weddings may have been three decades apart, their backgrounds and childhoods could not have been more different, and the courtships before their marriages were polar opposites. But the appearance of a new fresh-faced, attractive young bride marrying an heir to the throne has re-ignited memories of Diana, for whom the public's love has not faded.

Now, almost 14 years after her tragic death in a Paris car crash on August 31, 1997, Diana's memory is still fresh in the minds of millions, especially her sons William and Harry.

If she was still alive today she would be 50 years old on July 1, and we can only guess what twists and turns her life would have taken in the past decade.

But one thing is certain. The wedding of her eldest son, William, to the love of his life, Kate, would have been one of the happiest days of her life.

Always a champion of spontaneity and unstuffy ways, Diana would surely have loved the fresh, intimate touches they made to the pomp and circumstance of a royal wedding.

And, most of all, she would have loved the beaming smiles on their faces as they emerged hand-in-hand from Westminster Abbey.

Kate Middleton may have married the man that made her the future Queen. But on her wedding day, like Diana three decades before her, she was first and foremost a young bride in love.

Shy DI & CONFIDENT KATE

When it first emerged that they were in a relationship with the heir to the throne, Lady Diana Spencer and Kate Middleton had to adjust to the public spotlight as we got to know them. Their lives would never be the same again

Charles and the Blushing Lady

THURSDAY, SEPTEMBER 18, 1980

The spotlight turned on Prince Charles's latest girlfriend yesterday – and it made her blush.

Lady Diana Spencer, the 19-year-old girl who gossips claim could one day be Queen, said as she worked at a London kindergarten: "All this fuss is disrupting my work with the children."

Asked about Prince Charles, she said: "I will not say anything about Prince Charles. No one has told me to keep quiet – it's my decision."

She also denied she had taken advice from Buckingham Palace about how to handle publicity.

Later, Lady Diana, daughter of former Royal equerry Lord Spencer, admitted she was mildly embarrassed by one of the photographs taken at the kindergarten yesterday.

DAILY Mirror

Thursday, September 18, 1980   12p

Charles and the Blushing Lady

CHARLES: Courting

THE spotlight turned on Prince Charles's latest girlfriend yesterday —and it made her blush.

Lady Diana Spencer, the 19-year-old girl who gossips claim could one day be Queen, said as she worked at a London kindergarten: "All this fuss is disrupting my work with the children."

Asked about Prince Charles she said: "I will not say anything about Prince Charles. No one has told me to keep quiet — it's my decision."

She also denied she had taken advice from Buckingham Palace about how to handle publicity.

Later, Lady Diana, daughter of former Royal equerry Lord Spencer, admitted she was mildly embarrassed by one of the photographs taken at the kindergarten yesterday.

"I was so nervous about the whole thing I never thought I'd be standing with the light right behind me," she said. "I don't want to be remembered for not having a petticoat."

Spanish holiday tragedy

By JACK PILER

A KILLER virus has struck down Britons returning from a holiday on Spain's Costa Blanca.

A 41-year-old father of two has died and five other Britons are seriously ill after staying at a hotel in Benidorm.

At least 800 Britons are still at the hotel, which has a history of attacks by the virus, known as Legionnaire's Disease.

Last night Thomson Holidays, main users of the 456-room Rio Park Hotel in the centre of the resort, were hurriedly moving trippers to other hotels.

BRITONS HIT BY KILLER VIR...

Refund

Holidaymakers due to fly out this weekend will be offered an alternative hotel, or a refund if they cancel.

A team of doctors from London was flying out to work with Spanish medical authorities.

The mystery illness — a type of pneumonia — was not diagnosed until the Britons arrived home. The dead man came from Manchester. The five survivors—from Oxford, Bedford, Manchester, Birmingham and Liverpool—are making a good recovery.

The first outbreak of the virus at the Rio Park Hotel was in 1973, when three British holidaymakers died.

Another Briton died in 1977, and in 1973 two cases were reported involving Britons who had stayed there, but both recovered.

The hotel was investigated and given a clean bill of health.

The tough... top with S... read JOHN ...—SEE P...

DAILY Mirror
Friday April 2 2004

GRAND NATIONAL

NEWSPAPER OF THE YEAR   35p

FREE £2 BET
SEE PAGE 15

CORAL™ INTERNET ONLY

WILLS IS SO FIT

By JANE KERR, Royal Reporter

PRINCE William's girlfriend Kate Middleton fancied him before they even met, friends revealed yesterday.

When the 21-year-old found out that she would be studying with the heir to the throne at university, she declared: "I think he's fit."

Wills and Kate are now living together as a couple at a cottage near St Andrews in Fife.

One of her friends said last night: "We always said they'd end up getting together. You could tell she really liked him. She is just perfect for the prince."

FULL STORY: PAGES 4 & 5

EXCLUSIVE: Prince's first love on her man

Lady Di's childhood photo album

TUESDAY, JUNE 30, 1981   **By Marje Proops**

When Lady Diana Spencer was a chubby, cuddly three-year-old, it must have been apparent to those who study such matters that here was a young lady with considerable potential for looks and character.

Of all those enchanting pictures of Prince Charles's bride-to-be released by Buckingham Palace on the eve of her 20th birthday tomorrow, the three-year-old chubby chops is my favourite. From this endearing toddler has developed the girl who has an adoring nation at her none-too-dainty feet.

The nicest thing about Lady Di growing up is how naturally and unselfconsciously she appears to have done it, despite the background of wealth and privilege into which she was born. There's shy Lady Di, cheeky Lady Di, mischievous Lady Di, a Lady Di showing a touch of defiance as she marches along with her pram, and certainly a Lady Di who is plainly a bit apprehensive – of her small pony.

But nowhere is there the slightest hint of a snooty, upper class Lady Di. Upper class she certainly is but it's because of her friendly, casual simplicity that she's knocked us all for six.

As she leaves her carefree teens she knows she's got a tough life ahead. She'll need all that well-known good humour and that touch of mischief which punctuates her growing-up pictures. Few will envy her dedicated future. But many will envy Prince Charles, who has got himself a pretty special and – for one still so young – an amazingly mature girl.

Rosy cheeks: A selection of images of Lady Diana Spencer as she grew up

Cute: The Daily Mirror puts the focus on a young Kate Middleton

"There was always something about her"

THURSDAY, MAY 5, 2011

The wedding of Kate Middleton and Prince William was the end of an extraordinary journey for the middle-class girl who once played Eliza Doolittle in a production of My Fair Lady, and the start of a new life as the future Queen of England.

The girl who will one day live in Buckingham Palace, spent her earliest years in a Victorian semi in Bradfield Southend, Berkshire. Born on January 9, 1982, Kate was a first child for Carole, 27 and Michael, 32.

When Carole and Michael met, she was a British Airways air hostess and he a flight-dispatcher for the same airline. They married in 1980, in the quiet village of Dorney, Bucks.

Soon after their second daughter Pippa was born, Michael was promoted to become a manager for British Airways and in May 1984, the family moved to Amman, the capital of Jordan in the Middle East. They lived in a three-bedroom villa and in 1985 Kate went to the Al-Sahera Kindergarten. She learned numbers, colours and her first nursery rhymes in Arabic, as well as English.

In 1986, they moved to Berkshire when Carole was pregnant with Kate's little brother, James, born in April 1987. Despite being a busy mum, Carole noticed a gap in the market for children's party products and set up her own mail-order company called Party Pieces. It began to flourish – current estimates value the firm at £30million.

The children were enrolled in expensive private schools – Kate attended St Andrew's School in Pangbourne, which now costs up to £12,000 a year. Kate's former PE teacher Denise Allford said: "I know it's easy to say it now, but there was always something about her. She wasn't particularly pretty as a young girl and she wore braces on her teeth from the age of 12. She was thin and much taller than the other girls – quite gangly, really. Her sister Pippa was the more beautiful at that age. But Catherine was very determined, which seemed to set her apart."

Kate blossomed, excelling at sport. When she was 11, she took the starring role of Eliza Doolittle in a production of My Fair Lady. She left the school with a prize for "all-round effort and pleasantness" but the next period of Kate's education was less enjoyable. The Middletons moved from their semi to a five-bedroom detached home with acres of land in Bucklebury, Berks. Kate became a day girl at the nearby £30,000-a-year Downe House School. But she was bullied for being too nice.

Shy Kate was moved after two terms to mixed boarding school Marlborough College in Wiltshire, and once again thrived. Friends have told how Kate rarely joined in when everyone was getting drunk and was often assigned to look out for teachers.

But despite her good-nature, Kate was not considered "a babe" by the boys until she returned to study A-Level chemistry, biology and art. The "nerd" was now "the most fancied girl in school", but she had few love interests. Classmate Gemma Williamson said: "Kate had a couple of innocent snogs but never had a boyfriend. She had enough strength of character not to care if the other girls thought her prudish. I got the distinct impression that Kate wanted to save herself for someone special."

We used to tell her: 'You'll be Queen one day'

FRIDAY, APRIL 5, 2004

Friends of Kate Middleton last night told how they were certain Prince William would not be able to resist her beauty and charm.

They even joked that she would be Queen one day after the sport-loving brunette confessed she fancied the young royal.

History of art student Kate, 21, worked as a deckhand on the BT Global Challenge yacht before heading to St Andrews University, where she met boyfriend Wills. One of her former crewmates on the Southampton-based craft said: "Kate was gorgeous and very popular. She was from a good family and seemed just perfect for the prince.

"After the crew heard Kate and William were both going to St Andrews we said they'd end up getting together. We used to tell her: 'You'll be the Queen one day'. It was a long-running joke.

"She used to laugh along but you could tell she really liked him. She admitted: 'I do fancy Wills'. Kate was so beautiful, we were sure William would fall for her. She's a lovely girl, good luck to her."

Kate and second in line to the throne William, 21, now live together as a couple in a cottage near St Andrews, Fife. She has met Prince Charles several times and sources are convinced their relationship is "serious". Charles is understood to approve. The pair went to great lengths to keep their four-month-old romance a secret. Only close friends knew about the relationship, and were sworn to secrecy.

Old Etonian Fergus Boyd, who shares the cottage, was one of the few in the know. Every time Kate and Wills left the home they made it look as if they were nothing more than housemates.

In public they never held hands or showed affection to each other. Friends said William knew their secret would come out, but he wanted to keep it private for as long as possible.

Even yesterday, when photographs of the pair on a skiing holiday in Switzerland were published, the prince ordered Clarence House aides to keep quiet.

William and Kate met when they both began studying History of Art at St Andrews. The prince later switched to geography. At the beginning of their second year, Wills moved out of the halls of residence into a flat in the town with Kate and Fergus.

The trio moved into their cottage on the outskirts of the town last September. Speculation has surrounded the couple's friendship since 2002, although they have always denied being romantically involved.

William reportedly paid £200 for a VIP ticket to a university fashion show where she modelled a bra and knickers while wearing a see-through dress. At the May Day Ball last year, the prince spent most of the evening huddled up with Kate and other friends.

They were photographed walking together down the local high street, deep in conversation at a rugby game. William and Kate have much in common. Both like sport. They play tennis together, and she loves watching rugby and polo. She was on the sidelines to cheer on William when he played in a rugby sevens tournament. The pair both spent part of their gap year in Chile.

She has been credited with persuading William to stay at St Andrews after reports he wanted to quit because it was "boring".

Kate is discreet and loyal, qualities William counts on from his friends. Kate, who has a sister Phillippa, 19, and 16-year-old brother James, was educated at St Andrew's in Pangbourne, Berks, then Marlborough College in Wiltshire.

During university breaks Kate returns home to Bucklebury, near Newbury. She was among the 300 guests invited to William's 21st birthday party at Windsor Castle last June.

What would you buy Charles for his birthday?

FRIDAY, NOVEMBER 7, 1980

Hunched against the cold wind, a young woman sets out on a shopping trip in fashionable Kensington.

As Lady Diana Spencer – tipped as the girl most likely to marry Prince Charles – joined the crowds yesterday, there was one very important item on her shopping list.

Next Friday is Charles's 32nd birthday. So what do you buy the man who seems to have everything – including, one day, the throne of England?

If Lady Diana is impatient for him to pop the question, she might jog his memory with a subscription to Brides magazine. Or a ring catalogue from Bravingtons.

Wills loves Kate: It's official

TUESDAY, SEPTEMBER 20, 2005

Prince William and his girlfriend Kate Middleton are to step out together at an official public occasion for the first time.

They are planning to "come out" as a couple after becoming frustrated with the secrecy surrounding their relationship.

The move will finally make Kate and William an accepted item in the royal household and is the next step on the way to a possible engagement.

A Clarence House insider said last night: "William has grown weary of the cloak and dagger operation surrounding his girlfriend.

"He wants her to be acknowledged as an important part of his life. He is planning to appear in public with her as a statement of intent and commitment to her. William is very much in love with Kate and he does not understand why this should be a secret."

Aides so far refuse to admit publicly that 23-year-old Kate is even William's girlfriend.

But the prince – also 23 – wants her to be given the royal stamp of approval and has introduced her to the Queen.

I'd like to marry soon, says Lady Di

SATURDAY, NOVEMBER 29, 1980

Lady Diana Spencer admitted yesterday that she wants to marry soon—perhaps next year.

She said so amid growing speculation that she will be Prince Charles's bride in 1981.

Blonde, blue-eyed Lady Diana spoke frankly while at work in a London kindergarten. She wore a paint-spattered smock, and children played noisily around her.

"Yes, I'd like to marry soon," she said. "What woman doesn't want to marry eventually? Next year? Why not?"

She added that she loved children. "I don't think 19 is too young," she said. "It depends on the person."

Nor did she think age difference mattered. The Prince is 32.

Asked if Charles had proposed, she blushed and giggled. "I can't confirm or deny it," she said. "I never talk about Charles."

Of the story claiming that she spent several hours on the royal train with the Prince, she said: "I want to get the record straight. The story was completely false.

"I was not on the royal train when they said and have never been on it. I don't even know what it looks like." The Sunday Mirror claimed that Lady Diana was smuggled aboard the train in Wiltshire sidings on November 5.

Sunday Mirror editor Robert Edwards said last night: "I made a gentleman's agreement with Mr Michael Shea, the Queen's Press secretary, to publish the correspondence between us in last week's paper and leave it at that.

"I am very sorry if Lady Diana has been upset by our report. By all accounts she's an extremely nice girl."

The Prince, who is touring India, joked yesterday: "I might just take the Muslim religion and have lots of wives. That would be more fun."

WILLS ENDED IT BY PHONE

SPLIT: William and, right, ex Kate

Revealed.. final call to Kate in a car park

EXCLUSIVE
By GRAHAM BROUGH

PRINCE William confirmed to stricken Kate Middleton that their romance was over in a dramatic mobile phone call.

Kate, 25, was hoping for a reconciliation even though she and Wills, 24, agreed at an Easter meeting their four-year affair was on the rocks.

A colleague who saw her take the call in a car park at her work in London, said: "It was clear it was William – and definitely a tiff."

FULL STORY: PAGES 4 AND 5

The strain shows: Pictured together just weeks before they broke up in 2007

Nursing a broken heart

MONDAY, APRIL 16, 2007

Kate Middleton bravely kept her heartbreak secret after Prince William confirmed their four-year romance was over in a tense phone call.

She was hurting so much inside she had to leave work and has not been seen there since. But there were no public tears. The couple had previously agreed to end their affair in an amicable Easter meeting.

A workmate witnessed Kate, 25, take Wills's dramatic call on her mobile phone on Wednesday after arriving for work looking "subdued, but okay". The colleague disclosed: "Around the middle of the day, she was pacing the car park outside the office on her mobile.

"A few people noticed because it's a pretty unusual thing to do. She'd deliberately gone outside to take the call because she didn't want to be overheard. Kate was walking up and down and looking upset, as if she was having an argument. But she didn't cry. It was clear that she was talking to William on the phone, because her behaviour was so unusual.

"When she came back to the office she didn't say a thing and disappeared for the rest of the day. She hasn't been back to work since. When someone asked where she was, they were told she was sick. Yet she hasn't been marked sick in the book. We didn't think anything about it at the time. But looking back, the call was definitely a girlfriend-boyfriend tiff."

Yesterday, Kate was nursing her broken heart at her parents' house near Newbury, Berks. She went out alone for a quiet drive in her silver Audi, then joined mum Carole, 50, dad Michael and 22-year-old sister Pippa for lunch.

Kate, a buyer at fashion chain Jigsaw based in Kew, south west London, was dressed in skinny jeans and a casual shirt. She hid her eyes behind dark glasses.

William, 24 – who partied on Friday night as the break-up became public – spent the weekend alone at Highgrove.

The couple had a heart to heart over the Easter weekend when they admitted their relationship was on the rocks.

William told Kate of his frustration that he could not fully concentrate on his new life as a young officer. Nor did he feel free to enjoy himself. He knows he faces increasing commitments as he takes on a more senior role in the Royal family. He now believes his two years in the Army could be his last chance for fun.

Kate told him she felt abandoned by his long hours with the Army, and did not want to be treated like a doormat.

Sources close to the couple insisted the break-up was amicable and said they would remain friends. Courtiers have not ruled out the possibility of them being reunited in a few years.

Still smiling: At the Badminton horse trials in May 2007. On the opposite page, she is seen enjoying herself at Twickenham and the Cheltenham horse racing festival

Together again: Sat apart at the Concert for Diana in July 2007, but their romance was about to be rekindled. Over the following 12 months Kate had plenty to smile about, joining William as he received his RAF wings, sharing a joke with Harry and enjoying the tennis at Wimbledon (all below). On the opposite page, the lovebirds dance at William's 26th birthday party

Thrills and Kate

TUESDAY, JULY 3, 2007

Prince William and Kate Middleton stunned revellers at the Diana concert after-show party with a passionate smooch on the dance floor.

They celebrated the rekindling of their romance with a raunchy routine that had VIP guests whooping with delight.

At one point revellers looked on open-mouthed as Wills brazenly gave Kate's boobs a loving squeeze while the couple – both 25 – rocked to R'n'B grooves.

Hugging and kissing, Wills and Kate weren't shy about letting the world know their romance is back on. They began the night in separate corners, but as the dance floor filled, they began to make their moves.

As the Dom Perignon, lychee martinis and other cocktails flowed, Wills and Kate both received plenty of attention from wannabe suitors. The prince made a point of chatting to pop beauty Joss Stone for 15 minutes – right in Kate's eyeline.

At one point Kate hissed to a pal: "He's ignoring me!" She then took to the dance floor, showing off her toned figure in a clingy white lace minidress. She was soon surrounded by male admirers as superstar DJ Erick Morillo pumped up the volume.

Suddenly a sweat-drenched Wills made his move. Waving one hand in the air, jumping up and down to the pounding music, the future king grabbed Kate and planted a smacker on her lips.

The reunited couple kissed passionately over two Mojito cocktails.

Rock 'n' royal

MONDAY, JUNE 6, 2008

Party-loving Prince William hurls his arms in the air and sings his heart out as he celebrates his 26th birthday.

Our exclusive pictures prove Wills is a Royal who really does love to let his heir down as he twirls giggling girlfriend Kate Middleton during a boozy celebration.

He began the evening sedately enough, quietly drinking and chatting with Kate, brother Harry and a few friends at the annual Beaufort Polo Club party.

But once the music began to blare, Wills could not resist the temptation to grab Kate and haul her on to the dance floor in a huge tent on the club grounds.

He put in a couple of requests with the DJ – and as a string of hits by Nickleback, Rhianna, Bon Jovi and AC/DC began playing, the prince started to show off his fancy footwork. Even the faithful Kate, 26, could not suppress her giggles as the prince gyrated about, throwing his arms aloft in what appeared to be an impression of a helicopter attempting to land.

But he was not going to let her get away with being a spectator – and Wills was soon whisking Kate around the floor as he laughed out loud. When the music finally slowed, he showed a more tender side – pulling her in close for a slow dance.

JOINED BY A RING

After frenzied speculation, the engagement announcements increased the attention on the royal couples. Poignantly, William presented Kate with the same ring worn by his mother when she and Charles were engaged in 1981

"I never had any doubts," says Lady Diana

WEDNESDAY, FEBRUARY 25, 1981

Prince Charles told yesterday of the night he popped the question to bride-to-be Lady Diana Spencer.

His proposal came as the couple sat down to dinner in the sitting room of the Prince's private quarters in Buckingham Palace. They got together for their romantic meeting "two or three days" before Lady Diana went on holiday to Australia on February 6.

Yesterday, in the same sitting room and with Lady Diana by his side, the Prince said: "I wanted to give Diana a chance to think about it, to think if it was going to be too awful." At that point Lady Diana chipped in: "Oh, no. I never had any doubts about it."

Although many have suggested that Prince Charles and Lady Diana have known each other since childhood, neither can remember meeting before 1977, the year of the Queen's silver Jubilee.

Lady Diana said: "Charles came to a shoot and we met in the middle of a ploughed field. He was really a friend of my sister, Lady Sarah then." Prince Charles said: "I remember a very jolly, amusing and bouncy 16-year-old. She was very attractive, great fun and full of life." Lady Diana's first impression of Prince Charles? "Pretty amazing."

They began to fall in love at Balmoral last July when Lady Diana went there to help her sister Lady Jane – married to Robert Fellowes, the Queen's assistant private secretary, with Jane's first baby.

Prince Charles and Diana walked through the romantic Highland scenery together, and she watched him fish for salmon in the River Dee. "We began to realise then that there was something in it," said Charles. He said the wedding date would be some time late in July, but they were still debating where the wedding would take place.

They exchanged affectionate glances as they talked, but Lady Diana maintained a shy poise and left her husband-to-be to conduct most of the interview. But one thing she did make clear was that the difference of just over 12 years in their ages did not matter. "I have never thought about the age gap." The Prince said: "Diana will certainly keep me young – you are only as old as you think you are."

The Prince said he was sure that Lady Diana would make a very good Princess of Wales. "She will be 20 soon and I was about that age when I started. It's obviously difficult to start with, but you just have to plunge in." Lady Diana was more cautious. "I will just take it as it comes," she said.

Prince Charles and Lady Diana feel they have a lot in common. "Diana is a great outdoor-loving sort of person," he said.

Lady Diana said: "We both love music and dancing, and we both have the same sense of humour."

"You'll definitely need that," said the Prince with a laugh.

Lady Diana, although only 19, seemed poised and confident as she sat beside the Prince, but she conceded it was "marvellous" to have his moral support.

Talking about Charles's proposal, she said: "Actually I said 'Yes' quite promptly. I had had a long time to think about it and it was not a difficult decision in the end."

How do the couple feel now that the world knows about their romance? "Thrilled," they said together. "Just delighted and happy," added Prince Charles.

To the inquiry "And in love?" Lady Diana replied: "Of course."

Lady Diana was asked whether she thought she could stand up to the pressures and responsibilities of being married to the future King.

She replied: "I have had a run up to it all in the last six months. Prince Charles will be there with me."

Have the last few months been a strain?

"Anyone in the position we have been in would have been under pressure. I hope I coped with it," said Lady Diana. Prince Charles added: "I am amazed she has been brave enough to take me on."

DAILY Mirror

nesday, February 25, 1981   12p

HIS ROYAL HIGHNESS THE PRINCE OF WALES PRESENTS:

MY DI

SOUVENIR ISSUE
PLEASE TURN TO BACK PAGE
ALSO PAGES 2, 3, 7, 15, 16 AND 17

Lady Di:
"I have never thought about the age gap…"

Charles:
"Diana will certainly keep me young …"

DAILY Mirror

Wednesday November 17, 2010

Kate

ROYAL NEWS.. ROYAL ENTERTAINMENT   45p

FREE INSIDE
8-page royal engagement souvenir edition

WITH THIS RING ..DI THEE WED

By MARTIN FRICKER

IT'S a sparkling moment of royal history – and a touching tribute from a son to his beloved mum.

Kate Middleton shows off Princess Diana's engagement ring as she and Prince William announce they are to wed.

William carried the priceless ring around in his rucksack for three weeks before proposing in Kenya last month.

"It's very special to me," he said. "As Kate's very special to me now, it was right to put the two together."

Kate said Diana was an "inspirational woman" and that becoming a royal was a "daunting prospect". The couple, both 28, will marry next year after eight years together.

FULL STORY INSIDE

◄ HAPPY DI
Kate wears Diana's ring

It's official: The photocalls after the engagements were announced. Below, stills from the joint television interview given by William and Kate

Di do!

WEDNESDAY, NOVEMBER 17, 2010

Prince William told how he gave Kate Middleton his late mother's engagement ring in poignant tribute to her.

William hid Diana's 18-carat blue sapphire in his rucksack on their holiday to Africa – and admitted he was terrified of losing it.

He chose a secluded spot near Mt Kenya to pop the question, and slipped the ring on to her finger. Tellingly, it was a perfect fit.

The prince, 28, said: "It is my mother's engagement ring. It is very special to me and Kate is very special to me now as well. It is only right the two are put together. It is my way of making sure my mother didn't miss out on today."

He revealed they had "been talking about marriage for a while". He said: "The timing is right, now. We are both very, very happy." He would not reveal whether he had gone down on one knee. Kate, also 28, would only say: "It was very romantic and it was very personal."

The couple's joy was obvious in an interview with ITV News.

Q: *Where did you propose, when, how and Kate, what did you say?*
WILLIAM: About three weeks ago. We had private time away with some friends and I just decided it was the right time. We had been talking about marriage for a while, so it wasn't a big surprise.

KATE: It was very romantic. There's a true romantic in there.

Q: *And you knew you were going to do this from day one of the holiday or did you wait until the end?*

WILLIAM: I'd been planning it for a while but as any guy will know it takes a certain amount of motivation to get yourself going. I was planning it and it felt really right in Africa. It was beautiful at the time. I had done a little bit of planning to show my romantic side.

Q: *And produced a ring there?*

WILLIAM: Yes. I had been carrying it around with me in my rucksack and I literally would not let it go because I knew if it disappeared, I would be in a lot of trouble.

Q: *It's a family ring?*

WILLIAM: Yes. It's my mother's engagement ring so I thought it was quite nice because obviously she's not going to be around to share any of the fun and excitement of it all. This was my way of keeping her close to it all.

KATE: It's beautiful. I just hope I look after it. It's very, very special.

Q: *William's mother was this massive iconic figure. Is that intimidating?*

KATE: I would have loved to have met her and she's obviously an inspirational woman to look up to.

WILLIAM: No one is trying to fill my mother's shoes. What she did was fantastic. It's about making your own future and your own destiny and Kate will do a good job of that.

William and Kate met at St Andrews University in 2002. They were friends for a year and even shared a flat with pals before falling in love. William revealed: "We spent more time with each other, had lots of fun and realised we shared the same interests.

"She's got a really naughty sense of humour, which helps me because I've got a really dry sense of humour, so it was good fun. We had a really good laugh and things happened."

Asked if they had known from the start that they would wed, he said: "When I first met Kate, I knew there was something special about her."

His fiancée admitted she went "bright red" when they were introduced. Asked about stories that she had his picture on her bedroom wall as a teenager, she laughed: "He wishes. No, I had the Levi's guy."

STEPPING OUT
As a ROYAL

After the engagements had been announced, Diana and Kate undertook their first official duties alongside their fiancées. Both women were now the centre of attention as royal wedding fever began to take hold

A royal meeting: Diana pictured with Princess Grace of Monaco at a concert in aid of the Royal Opera House at Goldsmiths' Hall, March 1981

Lady Di takes the plunge

TUESDAY, MARCH 10, 1981

Glamorous Lady Diana Spencer stole the show last night when Prince Charles proudly escorted her on their first public engagement.

Her black off-the-shoulder evening dress with a plunging neckline delighted a crowd of about 200 who watched her arriving at Goldsmiths' Hall in the City of London.

But the classic effect of severe black silk and white skin was relieved with a splash of colour when she was presented with a red rose by Liberal MP Cyril Smith.

That pleased the photographers – and her diamond necklace bracelet and earrings sparkled as the flashbulbs popped.

Lady Diana looked relaxed and happy on her first public appearance as Charles's fiancée…until the slight drizzle started to reach her.

Then she slipped on a matching silk coat. Prince Charles, obviously aware of the stir his bride-to-be was causing, grinned at the photographers and asked: "Have all the fashion writers finished?"

Then he whisked her off inside the building to hear a verse-and-music presentation in aid of the Royal Opera House development fund.

One of the poetry reciters was Princess Grace of Monaco, who congratulated Charles on his engagement.

Normally Princess Grace, formerly the actress Grace Kelly, is the centre of attention. But last night belonged to Lady Diana.

Jewel on her finger: Kate at a Teenage Cancer Trust Christmas spectacular while, right, she attends a wedding of friends in January 2011

CENTRE STAGE

With Charles at Royal Ascot (above), at Balmoral (right) and sharing a carriage with Prince Andrew during Trooping the Colour (below).

Kate's a corker

FRIDAY, FEBRUARY 25, 2011

Glamorous Kate Middleton sparkled at her first official engagement yesterday.

Looking stylish in a tweed coat, Kate launched a new lifeboat with champagne as hubby-to-be Prince William joked: "She gets to do the fun bit."

Crowds lining the street cheered "Kate, Kate" as the couple arrived at Trearddur Bay lifeboat station in Anglesey — where they have their North Wales home.

Wills, 28, greeted the crowd in Welsh, apologising for his "terrible pronunciation". And as RNLI craft Hereford Endeavour was launched, the prince — a search and rescue helicopter pilot — said: "I realise, as we all do at RAF Valley, what a vital part this lifeboat plays in our combined effort to save people from the sea."

Kate, 29, sang Welsh anthem Land Of My Fathers word-perfectly and smiled for three hours of "meet and greet".

"It's been incredible," she said.

The pair will today launch St Andrews University's 600th anniversary charity appeal, then fly to London to sign a New Zealand earthquake condolences book.

Where they fell in love

SATURDAY, FEBRUARY 26, 2011

For their second royal engagement, Prince William and his fiancée Kate Middleton yesterday returned to the place they first met – St Andrews.

At the Scottish university, they chatted with students, professors and even their old cleaner. Kate, 29, who looked stunning in a striking scarlet and black outfit, and William were back at their former student haunt to launch the St Andrews' 600th anniversary charity appeal.

William, 28, who has been made patron of the charity, told the audience: "This is a very special moment for Catherine and me. It feels like coming home." Referring to the wild parties of his student days, he then joked: "It feels like we have a good chance of recreating Raisin Sunday today."

As an early wedding present to the couple, St Andrews launched a scholarship yesterday to give a student from a poor background the chance to study there. After their visit, Kate and William went to the centre of Fife, where they were met by a cheering crowd.

It appeared as if most of the town had turned out to see their famous former residents. As the couple stopped to chat and shake hands with the public, Kate revealed she is trying hard to keep pace with royal life. Glancing over at her fiancé, she said: "I have to try and keep up with him. He's always faster than me."

Kate was heard saying, "It's good to be back", and was greeted by smiles and bunches of flowers.

Happy memories: William and Kate return to St Andrews University. They met here after both enrolled on the art history course in 2001

Kate in a state

Dazzling: Entertaining the crowds while on official duties in Northern Ireland and Darwen, Lancashire

TUESDAY, APRIL 12, 2011

Getting married in front of two billion people would make anyone a bit jittery. Kate Middleton confessed as much yesterday to a well-wisher as she and William made their final public appearance before tying the knot.

Looking stunning in a navy suit and chunky heels, she told fans she could not believe the date had come around so soon.

And as the crowds clamoured to meet her and shake her hand, Asda worker Amanda Wood managed to get Kate to open up about walking down the aisle of Westminster Abbey on April 29.

The 46-year-old revealed: "I asked her if she was nervous about her wedding. And she said 'Yes, of course I am'. Then I told her she's beautiful."

Tens of thousands of people will line the streets of London, and a global audience will be glued to their TVs when she gets married in 17 days' time.

It was only a week ago Prince William admitted he was also a bit jumpy about the big day.

Wills, 28, revealed his knees were "tapping" during a rehearsal for the wedding. When asked what part he was nervous about, he joked: "The whole thing."

Kate, 29, was looking very slender yesterday as she and the prince arrived in the pouring rain to open Darwen Aldridge Community Academy in Darwen, Lancs.

The weather brightened up for their afternoon visit to nearby Whitton Country Park in Blackburn, where Kate glowed in the spotlight as she waved a flag to start a student 100 metre race.

And as she made her way down the line of people desperate to shake her hand, she repeated her nervous excitement to elderly Blackburn couple Margaret and Alwyn Davis.

"We said hello", said Margaret, 79. "And I said to her: 'I wish you all the best with your wedding'. And she said: 'Yes I can't believe it's coming very soon now'."

Alwyn, 83, added: "We went to London to see William's parents marry in 1981. Kate and William are a lovely couple and we're very honoured they've come to this part of the country. It was a bit of a surprise when we found out."

Smiling, laughing and bending down to talk to children, Kate charmed the community as police in uniform and plain clothes controlled the excited crowds. Three-year-old Isla Yardley was at the afternoon visit with her grandmother Sandra Hubbersley. Sandra said: "She touched Isla's pigtails. She's so tactile. It's lovely when they make an effort."

Julie Turnbull, 47, her daughter Janie Barnard, 24, and her two children Jodie and Kian Duckworth, five and three, waited patiently by the side of the road for two-and-a-half hours to get a glimpse of the royal couple at their morning engagement.

Julie said: "I've taken the day off work to be here today because it's the chance of a lifetime."

A total of 5,000 people turned out to see William and Kate. And they encouraged the couple to take up the county's local traditions by presenting Kate with a "courting cake". The heart-shaped shortbread with a raspberry jam centre is traditionally made by the bride and presented to the groom.

Kate and William's visits were their first public appearances in England after previous visits to Belfast, St Andrews and Anglesey.

Just one month ago, on an engagement in Belfast, Kate told a member of the crowd she's on a wedding diet. Well-wisher Heather Lindsay, 47, said she told her not to lose any more weight, and the bride-to-be revealed it was "all part of the wedding plan".

TWO DAYS
that captivated a
NATION

On two days almost 30 years apart, Britain ground to a halt to share in the joy of a royal wedding. Relive these unforgettable occasions when all the talk was of romance, dresses and kisses

The build-up: Three days before their nuptials, Charles and Diana are pictured at a polo match. Shortly before their wedding, William and Kate visited Diana's grave

I shall, I think, spend half the time in tears, said Charles

WEDNESDAY, JULY 29, 1981

Prince Charles hopes the wedding will be a "marvellous musical and emotional experience".

In last night's television interview with him and Lady Diana Spencer, he said he had always longed for a musical wedding. One hymn he had chosen – Christ is Made the Sure Foundation – had marvellous harmony, he said. The Prince added: "I find it very moving. I shall, I think, spend half the time in tears."

Lady Diana revealed that she intended to be "tucked up in bed" early last night. They had decided to follow the tradition that the bride and groom should not meet on the evening before the wedding. Lady Diana joked: "We might quarrel."

In the recorded interview with Angela Rippon of the BBC and Andrew Gardner of ITV, Lady Diana said she was looking forward to being a good wife.

She revealed she had done a cookery course but described herself only as an "average" cook. Turning to Prince Charles, she added: "But you haven't tasted anything, 'cos I won't let you!"

Prince Charles said he and Lady Diana loved St Paul's. He added: "One of the reasons I particularly wanted to be married at St Paul's is because I think that, musically speaking, it is such a magnificent setting, and the whole acoustics are so spectacular... I've taken a lot of interest in that and actually the whole thing."

The Prince added: "We've had a marvellous time getting together three orchestras that I'm patron of, and it is also exciting that Dame Kiri Te Kanawa, the opera singer, is prepared to sing in the cathedral.

The Prince said it was necessary to have "stirring, dramatic and noisy" music to "carry" him and Lady Diana down the aisle – a three-and-a-half minute walk.

Lady Diana said she had chosen one of the hymns for the service 'I Vow to Thee My Country', her favourite since her schooldays.

Asked if they had been able to put any small personal touches to make it their day, even though it was regarded as a State occasion, Lady Diana replied: "I think by inviting one's friends and all the people who've helped us."

Prince Charles then spoke of the problems of knowing there are "cameras poking at you from every quarter and recording every twitch you make". He said: "I think if you don't try to work out in your own mind some kind of method for existing and surviving this kind of thing, you would go mad."

Then he asked Lady Diana: "Do you find that after the last six months you're beginning to get used to it?" She replied: "Just."

Lady Diana said Prince Charles had been "a tower of strength" in helping her to adjust. But when he expressed surprise, she joked: "I had to say that because you're sitting there."

Prince Charles said that since the engagement was announced he had never seen such friendliness and generosity from people.

He said he and Lady Diana had received endless cards and presents and they had encountered "the most marvellous, warm, affectionate reaction, which I just find incredibly touching."

And she said: "It's been a tremendous boost, just a mass of smiling faces; it's wonderful."

Since their engagement, they had received about 100,000 letters and more than 3,000 presents.

Lady Diana said she had been particularly touched by all the gifts from children, who had spent hours of work on paintings, cards and baking cakes. Describing one cake, she said: "There are so many Smarties you can hardly see what it is. And it's lovely, very nice."

Asked about her interests, she said: "Well, obviously it's children, but interests will broaden as the years go on. As I'm 20, I've got a good start."

Wish me luck: Kate, accompanied by sister Pippa, arrives at the Goring Hotel, where she stayed on the eve of the wedding

Orf with his bed

WEDNESDAY, APRIL 27, 2011

They have been side by side for weeks, enthralling crowds as a couple head over heels in love preparing for their big day.

But yesterday, Prince William and Kate Middleton went their separate ways to spend their last days as singletons apart.

After a cosy Easter weekend together at Kate's parents' house, the couple said an emotional goodbye. They then headed off to different homes, knowing they would not see each other again until the bride walks up the aisle at Westminster Abbey on Friday, to be reunited with her groom.

The separation will have been a wrench for William, 28, who knows his support for Kate has eased her nerves in the run up to the wedding, which will be watched by two billion people around the globe. He will spend the next two days at his London home Clarence House, and is expected to spend a "quiet" last night as a bachelor with brother Harry, his best man.

Kate will stay with her parents Carole and Michael before heading to the Goring Hotel in Mayfair on the eve of the ceremony.

No doubt their separation will give them both time to contemplate the enormity of the day – and the excitement will turn to nerves.

The cleric who will be the first to meet Kate as she arrives at the Abbey insists the 29-year-old bride will be calm before the wedding. Dean of Westminster, the Very Reverend Dr John Hall, said: "I'm not sure exactly what I will say to her.

"I suppose I might have to make up a joke or two. I think I will just welcome her and assure her that everyone is with her, that's one of the key things.

"The congregation is made up of people who will be thrilled to be here. I feel she will have a sense of calmness.

"I'm sure there will be a great sense of excitement. It's important that she enjoys it. It's important William enjoys it."

William, who has admitted his knees have been "tapping" as the big day approaches, yesterday drove himself out of the driveway of the Middletons' £1million home in Bucklebury, Berkshire, at 9am to head for London.

Just six hours later Kate also drove herself and sister Pippa in her black Audi out of the house – returning within 45 minutes. It is believed Kate was making some final wedding arrangements with close friends, and picking up some last-minute items from local shops.

Spirit of Diana looms large but this is Kate's day

FRIDAY, APRIL 29, 2011   **By James Whitaker**

It was slightly scary – for me, if not for Kate Middleton – when Prince William proposed using his mother Diana's engagement ring.

To begin with I thought 'how enchanting, how romantic, what a beautiful gesture'. Then I began to have doubts. That maybe a teeny, weeny bit too much of the mother-in-law Kate will never meet was creeping into this beautiful day.

My fears increased yesterday when I read the Order of Service, put out by St James's Palace, in advance of today's great occasion at Westminster Abbey.

The spirit of Diana was looming large on day one of the engagement announcement last November, and it's still here on the day of the marriage itself.

Great for William and his brother Harry, who vowed never to forget their mother, but maybe not so great for the bride herself.

Of course, I feel sure Kate and Diana would have loved one another and got on like a house on fire.

I have no doubt that the Princess of Wales would have been immensely proud of the woman Wills has chosen to live with for the rest of his life.

But the opening hymn of the service at the Abbey today is Guide Me, O Thou Great Redeemer.

It's a beautiful enough anthem that can kick-start any indolent heart.

But it's also the very same hymn that was the final one at Princess Diana's funeral – inside Westminster Abbey – in September 1997.

It was also played at The Guards Chapel at the service to mark the 10th anniversary of her death.

There will be other examples of the spirit of Princess Diana floating around us all today. Kate's bridal procession music as she walks towards the High Altar was also used in the 1981 marriage between William's mother and father.

There is more. Three other pieces of music or hymns from Prince Charles and Diana's wedding at St Paul's Cathedral will also be heard today.

Some may find it a wonderful tribute to a woman I personally thought was the bees' knees. But surely there must have been some misgivings within the Middleton camp?

I know the two lovebirds thought long and hard about the make-up of today's service, and intriguingly, Prince Charles himself is said to have had an input on the music.

Prince William, totally supported by brother Harry in thought and deed, is fulfilling the promise they made to the world a number of years ago – namely to think of their mother every single day and cherish and honour her memory until the day they die.

Laudable enough. And who could criticise such sentiments?

But I think it's possibly getting a little tough on Kate.

It may be our day, the Royal Family's day, the Middleton family's greatest ever day. But surely, rising above all others, this has to be Catherine's day – a woman we are learning to love more as each day goes by.

For my mum

FRIDAY, APRIL 29, 2011

Prince William and Kate Middleton will pay a touching tribute to Princess Diana today – when their wedding service will feature a hymn played at her funeral.

The couple have selected the final hymn from Diana's 1997 funeral, Guide Me, O Thou Great Redeemer, to be the first sung in Westminster Abbey by their guests.

Friends and family will join the royal couple to sing the inspiring words to the Welsh tune just before they say their vows in front of the Archbishop of Canterbury.

And in another tribute, bride Kate will make her three-and-a-half minute walk down the aisle to the dramatic sounds of Sir Hubert Parry's anthem I was Glad, which was played at Charles and Diana's wedding.

William has told close friends and royals he is sure his mother will be there in spirit today, wishing him and Kate happiness.

The last time William was in the Abbey

for a state occasion was after he was part of the slow and painful procession behind his mother's coffin, aged just 15.

William has said he gave Kate Diana's sapphire and diamond engagement ring as a way of "keeping her close to it all".

Kate spent hours listening to music on her iPod and also sought advice from Prince Charles. His hand can be seen in the inclusion of William Walton's Crown Imperial, which was played at the coronation of George VI – husband of his beloved late grandma, the Queen Mother.

There is also a strong nod to Wales in the couple's final musical decisions. Guide Me, O Thou Great Redeemer – from the Welsh tune by John Hughes with words by William Williams – is best known today as the Welsh rugby anthem Bread of Heaven. Love Divine, All Loves Excelling is set to the Welsh tune Blaenwern.

In honour of the North Wales island where they have set up home, William and Kate have also chosen a work by modern composer Paul Mealor, who has a studio on Anglesey.

But their final hymn is about as English as is possible – the stirring and popular Jerusalem, a poem by William Blake set to music by Sir Hubert Parry and arranged by Edward Elgar.

Here she is: With father Michael on the way to the ceremony, plus a final look back and wave as she enters Westminster Abbey

Her eyes danced with light like the diamonds of her tiara. She was gorgeous

THURSDAY, JULY 30, 1981

Diana was a silhouette at the West Door of St Paul's, covered in the white mystery of her veil. Over her head the frosty sparkle of diamonds was a glinting halo and the trumpets laid down a barrage.

She walked to her Prince and the people who were there gasped in the wake of her beauty.

Charles shuffled at his place but wasn't seen to look. The Queen bent her head and turned to look down the river of coarse red carpet. Prince Philip beamed a vast, happy smile and turned to Charles, whispering across the noisy space which was between them.

Wren's Dome curved over them and the light surged in through clear windows and everywhere there was a flourish of colour. Great cones of lilies stood either side of the dais and the pillars of St Paul's were looped with white daisies and yellow roses.

The old men, the Royal Ushers, leaned on the staffs of their pikes and stared towards Diana coming slowly on the arm of Earl Spencer, struggling in his sickness.

Charles turned to Prince Edward and waved him nearer to the place he had been told to stand. Philip nodded his approval and exchanged another happy message with his son.

Across from the Queen, Diana's grandmother, Lady Fermoy, watched with raging pride. Diana's mother, Mrs Shand-Kydd, looked over at the Queen Mother who smiled with her own enormous pride, and a warmth of friendliness passed between them.

Near the end of the fourth row in the body of the cathedral, Raine

The bride arrives: Arm-in-arm with her father, Earl Spencer, as she walks up the red carpet in St Paul's Cathedral, with a 25-foot train following her progress

Spencer, Diana's stepmother, weaved her head around the shoulders of the ranks of the bride's friends and families and caught rare glimpses of her.

But in this place, which nearly a thousand years ago had been known as the Temple of Diana, it was all about the new Diana and the Prince who was waiting.

Gold braid shone over Charles's shoulders and down his sash. The Orders of The Garter and The Thistle were glowing stars on his chest.

Under the misty wisps of her silk veil Diana smiled and the Cathedral glowed in the happiness which went out to greet her.

Diana came to Charles's side and he leaned to her and smiled his encouragement. They were embraced in their joy, which had always been there from the beginning of their love.

The last great chords of the Trumpet Voluntary soaked away into the shadowy chasms of the Cathedral and Diana smiled again and the secrecy of it behind her veil was part of her bewitchment.

Diana sang and she looked at her father who was giving the words the full vigour of his voice.

"Wilt thou have this woman to thy wedded wife?" the Archbishop of Canterbury said, when he moved in to take the service.

"I will," Charles said in a strong, sound voice and the words went out from those carpet-covered steps in St Paul's and were heard by one tenth of all the people in the world.

"I will," Diana replied when she was asked by the Archbishop.

The cheers battered against the doors from the street. They came too over the rooftops and down London's winding streets.

Charles began to beam. Diana's face was still hidden in what someone with a better view said was a blush.

She got his name wrong, Philip Charles instead of Charles Philip, and then scolded herself between replies by tightening her lips.

He blew it as well, leaving out "worldly" from "worldly goods".

The Royals followed Charles and Diana to the Dean's Aisle to sign the registers. Earl Spencer and Mrs Shand-Kydd followed. The Earl was at his shakiest when he returned.

Then it was Diana on Charles's arm with the veil swept from her face and her loveliness shining as the brightest sight in the spectacle of this day.

Her cheeks were toned with a girlish blush. Her eyes really danced with light like the diamonds of her tiara. She was gorgeous.

There was nothing more you could ask at the end of a fairy tale.

Head-turner: Pippa faithfully holds Kate's train
as she is greeted in the doorway of the Abbey.
Meanwhile, William waits and composes himself

So in love: The look in the eyes says it all

That dress and the train that took the strain

THURSDAY, JULY 30, 1981

The Princess's wedding dress will be as influential to bridal fashion in the years to come as her casual clothes have been during her four-month engagement.

She and her royal dressmakers, David and Elizabeth Emanuel, flouted simple, classic, easy-to-wear lines. She emerged from her coach at St Paul's in a vast crinoline of ivory silk paper taffeta, hand embroidered in tiny mother-of-pearl sequin and pearls, decorated elaborately with lace flounced sleeves and neckline, both decorated with taffeta bows.

The boned bodice nipped in her waist and accentuated many layers of ivory tulle that held the skirt of the dress out in ballgown style. As if this wasn't enough to contend with, she had a sweeping train 25-feet long in the same silk taffeta, trimmed and edged with sparkling lace and a veil of ivory tulle that was as long as her train.

She stepped out in handmade wedding slippers with a tiny heel and softly pointed toe, created by Clive Shilton.

Her bouquet literally cascaded from her hands — a shower of gardenias, golden roses and white orchids.

In case of rain the designers had thought of everything. They had made a wedding parasol in the same silk and lace.

In March, they asked Phillips, the fine art auctioneers, to look out for a 19th century parasol in a pagoda shape. Soon afterwards one was sent by a Wimbledon housewife, who found one in an old trunk in the bedroom of her Aunt Sybil's tiny cottage in Bideford, Devon.

Lady Diana bought it by private sale and the Emanuels recovered the parasol to match the wedding dress.

The 63-year-old housewife, who wishes to remain anonymous, said yesterday: "Aunt Sybil would have been very, very proud. She adored the Royal family."

In the event, the rain stayed away, but according to Victor Young, director of the bridal shops Pronuptia, everyone will want a wedding parasol.

He said: "I also expect an increase in the demand for crinolines, for sequins and pearls, which up to now have been considered very old fashioned. It would be very hard to copy the dress, because there is so much fabric…in the dress, in the train and in the underskirt. It would be impossible to produce at a reasonable price."

Kate walked down the aisle...and into history

SATURDAY, APRIL 30, 2011   **By Tony Parsons**

Kate Middleton came down the aisle of Westminster Abbey and one thing was abundantly clear – William is lucky to have her. So are we.

Kate came down the aisle a radiant, elegant vision of beauty – incredibly slowly, as though she had waited for this day a long time, and now somebody else could do the waiting.

William was dashing in the bright red tunic of the Irish Guards. It was only with the arrival of Kate that he seemed to lose his control, and become almost bashful with love. She looked stunning and he told her so. Harry grinned with admiration.

But this did not feel like a fairy tale. It could have felt that way, with the bride in her white dream of a dress, and William looking like Prince Charming all ready for the ball.

A fairy tale? No – this was a man and a woman who have loved each other for a long time. Who met when they were young and went their separate ways and then found their way back to each other. A man and a woman who were planning to spend their lives together.

All the ritual of grand state ceremony in a 900-year-old church could not disguise what we were seeing – the union of two people who are deeply in love.

The tension and the pressure was unimaginable. All through her arrival and the wedding vows, Kate was a picture of calm – the beautiful, serene centre in the eye of the hurricane.

People spoke of Diana. They remembered her wedding to Charles, almost 30 years ago. And I could never forget her funeral, 14 years ago, when William was 15 years old.

We remembered Diana because Kate is so clearly a star, and so obviously stepping into the same glaring spotlight that finally consumed Diana. But they are very different women. Diana was just about in her 20s when she wed Charles, her far older groom. Kate and William are the same age and she will be 30 in January.

Diana was a girl. Kate is a woman. And when things go a bit wrong – like a ring that doesn't quite fit – William is the half of the couple who is prone to blushing. Kate is just a few months older than William, but she sometimes seems much older than him.

Every one of us felt the presence of Princess Diana in Westminster. Perhaps it was just a collective memory, or perhaps it was something else. Yet her spirit was there, real or imagined. But if Diana was watching, she was smiling. And now, at last, she was surely at peace.

The union of Kate and William represented both the way we were, and the way we are.

We were in a church that is almost 1,000 years old. But we were there to watch the marriage of a man and a woman who met at university, and who have lived together before marriage.

Kate and William are a young couple who do not look so very different to thousands of young couples in our country.

Yes, he is the future king of England and she is the next global superstar, style icon and figure of obsession. But at the centre of it all was a bride and groom, grinning at each other and looking like their greatest dream had just come true.

Kate and William are true stars, and they have that combination of availability and distance that true stardom requires. The attention they are bound to receive will be unimaginable.

Perhaps history will see that she is more suited to her new role than him.

But to me they looked like a couple who will grow old together, and who will never stop loving each other.

The human touch

We've done it: The ceremonials are over; let the celebrations begin

THURSDAY, JULY 30, 1981   **By Marje Proops**

She muddled up his name and called him Philip Charles Arthur George as she made her solemn vows. He forgot the "worldly" when he was promising to share all his goods with her.

And those two little slips of the tongue gave this great ceremonial wedding the human touch that turns a formal Royal occasion into a happy and glorious one.

She was marrying the future King of England, but that didn't prevent her clutching his hand as they stood together before all those dignified clergymen.

Prince Charles, much more accustomed to concealing his feelings, was less demonstrative. I began to think he'd never kiss the bride. Not at any rate in public.

But just as I began to despair, they kissed on the Palace balcony while the huge ecstatic crowd sang, in best soccer-style tradition, You'll Never Walk Alone. It was as if Prince Charles had just scored a goal.

And it was just one more demonstration of how, from start to finish, the wedding of the century had, despite the weeks of planning, the meticulous regimentation of the immensely grand formality, somehow become an intimate family affair.

There's no doubt it was the bride's endearing qualities of simplicity, charm and lack of 'side' or of snobbery which made her wedding curiously un-Royal.

From the first glimpse of the bride as she rode with her father from Clarence House to St Paul's, you felt that underneath all that incredibly beautiful finery was an ordinary, excited, eager girl — not so different really from any other young bride.

Her dress lived up to all the romantic expectations and she did look like the fairy tale bride we'd expected to see. The Emanuels did her proud.

The ivory silk taffeta old lace dress was a dream which would have been a nightmare on a shorter, plumper girl. But for the tall bride, it added up to perfection.

Far too elaborate, agreed a couple of churlish men near me, but every woman I spoke to loved every inch, every flounce and every frill of it.

TIME TO CELEBRATE

Prince Charles, Michael Middleton, Prince Philip, Carole Middleton, the Queen and Camilla, Duchess of Cornwall watch the happy couple depart after the ceremony, while crowds throng The Mall and Buckingham Palace. On the opposite page, Kate beams as she and William emerge from the Abbey.

THE PROCESSIONS

The horse-drawn carriages carrying the newly-married royal couples pass through the streets of London en route to Buckingham Palace. There are plenty of waves for the thrilled well-wishers.

The first kiss

THURSDAY, JULY 30, 1981

This is the kiss that says: We are in love. Let's tell the world. The crowd outside Buckingham Palace went wild with delight. It was a scene of sheer magic.

The kiss that set the seal on their happiness came when the newly-weds stepped on to the Palace balcony.

The lace-curtained doors opened, they walked out, waved – and then Prince Charles lovingly kissed his bride's hand. She leaned across and kissed him on the lips.

There was no sign of the famous Lady Diana blush. Gone, too, was nervousness.

For five minutes the couple smiled and waved to the crowd, turning now and then to the Queen and her family.

The chanting went on and on: "Prin-cess Di, Prin-cess Di." "Good old Char-lie, we want Char-lie."

Bride and groom made three appearances. And every moment thrilled the thousands below.

And then he kissed her...

SATURDAY, APRIL 30, 2011

This was the tender moment the thousands of delirious well-wishers gathered outside Buckingham Palace had been waiting for.

Prince William and his bride Kate delighted the crowds and billions watching around the globe with a loving kiss.

Moments earlier, Kate had strolled on to the Palace balcony, took in the euphoric crowd below and exclaimed: "Wow."

Those gathered soon let them know what they hoped to see, begging William: "Kiss her, kiss her." He waited a few minutes before he turned to Kate and asked: "Are you ready? Okay, let's..."

At 1.27pm the prince kissed Kate full on the lips. The cheering from the 500,000 people crammed below the balcony and in the Mall reached a deafening crescendo.

The crowd chanted once more: "Kiss again, kiss again, kiss again." And the second in line to the throne did not disappoint.

According to the Mirror's lip-reader, William turned to Kate and said: "Let's give them another one, I love you." He leaned over for another "balcony moment", at 1.30pm, this time just lingering a little longer.

A moment in time: The official group photograph following the wedding of Charles and Diana. To the right, the newly-titled Prince and Princess of Wales head off on their honeymoon, boarding a train at Waterloo Station which headed for Romsey in Hampshire

We've had a great day

SATURDAY, APRIL 30, 2011

There was delight when William and Kate drove through the streets in Prince Charles's Aston Martin with JU5T WED on the plates. The earlier applause rippled from the gates of the Palace into the Mall where it became a flood of resounding approval from well-wishers the world over.

It soon felt as if the tide of goodwill for William and Kate had swept through the whole of London, including the million men, women and children lining the route.

She later declared it had been a "great day", adding, "I'm glad the weather held off."

Many in the crowd camped out all night to get a glimpse of the commoner destined to become Queen Catherine. Just two hours earlier, she had been plain Kate Middleton. Now she was standing at the Palace next to the Queen, a fully-fledged member of the Royal Family.

Before the wedding, Her Majesty honoured the couple with the titles Duke and Duchess of Cambridge.

Glowing with happiness Kate, who wore a tiara lent by the Queen and an ivory silk and lace dress by Sarah Burton, waved to her admirers gathered below the balcony.

The Queen was heard commenting on the wedding by TV crews as she went into the Palace. She said: "It was amazing."

Britain's finest military personnel turned out to mark the unique occasion.

Soldiers, airmen and sailors lined the route. William, 28, was resplendent in the scarlet uniform of the Irish Guards, where he is honorary colonel. His 26-year-old brother and best man Harry turned out in his Blues and Royals uniform.

But the most spectacular military moment came in the fly-past. Two formations of iconic RAF aircraft from the Second World War era, as well as modern jets, flew over the Palace at 1.30pm. A huge cheer erupted as each group of aircraft swept across the sky.

Joker Harry pointed out to Prince Philip that he was smaller than the bride, making his granddad laugh.

The wedding was a formal state occasion but Kate and William's fresh, unstuffy approach to the monarchy made it a day of surprises.

Having celebrated at a reception inside the Palace, the couple emerged at 3.45pm providing a moment that was a million miles away from the pomp and pageantry of Westminster Abbey, where they tied the knot hours earlier.

William drove his bride in the open-top blue Aston Martin decorated with red, white and blue ribbons. The car was lent to him by his dad and decked out for the occasion by Harry, with two balloons bearing the couple's initials W and C.

At the same time a Royal Navy Sea King helicopter flew low over the Queen Victoria Memorial in a surprise tribute to William's work as an RAF search and rescue pilot.

William and Kate later returned to the Palace for an evening reception with family and friends. The bride wore a strapless white dress with diamante detail, also made by Sarah Burton.

Ellie Goulding was due to serenade William and Kate at the party. The pop star was expected to sing Elton John's Your Song for the happy couple's first dance. Guest Sir Elton said: "It was a wonderful and glorious day."

A Di to remember

SATURDAY, APRIL 30, 2011   **By James Whitaker**

A touch of style: William and Kate delight the crowds by making the short journey from Buckingham Palace to Clarence House in a vintage Aston Martin. On the opposite page, the RAF fly-past has the couple gazing into the skies

I don't actually have tears in my eyes but I am drained emotionally by it all.

I've seen this before, from my front row seat at the wedding of William's mother and father. But although that day was more emotional and jaw-dropping, because it was the first of its kind, yesterday's was warmer.

From the moment Kate (we really should start calling her Catherine but of course we won't) emerged from The Goring hotel on the arm of her father, Michael Middleton, until she stood on the Buckingham Palace balcony, she had us eating out of her newly manicured hands.

And she judged the mood just right. She was confident without being cocky. She was knowing without being smug. She was, I have to admit, a triumph. We all saw a star being born as she held hands with her hubby while they kissed... twice!

William and Kate stood at the High Altar in the Abbey as equals. Not quite in status but certainly in each of their contributions to this glorious occasion.

Both bring a very great deal to this marriage and one got the feeling yesterday that the "we're in this together" will last. That certainly was not the case when Charles and Diana were married at St Paul's in 1981.

There were no cock-ups or mispronunciations, no waverings as each took their vows and no mistakes as the two made their way into and out of the Abbey.

William, as he was about to be betrothed, whispered to his about-to-be father-in-law: "We were supposed to have just a small family affair."

There was none of this casual banter at St Paul's in 1981. But somehow, maybe because Prince Charles was heir to the throne at the time whereas William is still only second in line, my memories of 30 years ago remain more evocative and colourful. It was a grander occasion and there was more pomp and circumstance.

So where do these two lovebirds go from here? Onwards and upwards, hopefully. They are a modern couple for a new(ish) century. And yesterday I saw a changing from the old guard to the new. If the monarchy has a future, Wills and Kate are it.

The new Duchess, courtesy of the new royal dukedom bestowed on William by his grandmother earlier in the day, was elegant, composed and, dare I say it, "regal".

She has much to learn and has a whole new life to get used to as the wife of the second-in-line to the throne.

But, by George, she made a great start.

THE *first* WOMAN IN WILLIAM'S LIFE

Long before he met Kate Middleton, there was only woman in Prince William's life: his mum.

Diana adored her eldest child, and the feeling was mutual. William honoured her in a very public way by presenting Kate with his mother's engagement ring. He explained: "It is very special to me. I thought it was quite nice because obviously she's not going to be around to share any of the fun and excitement of it all. This was my way of keeping her close to it all."

There was a great love between the two of them, forged in trying circumstances. Despite the rigid formalities and protocol that so often defines royal life, Diana did all she could to provide William and Harry with as normal an upbringing as possible, offering light and shade. They enjoyed fun days out at theme parks and she took them to homeless shelters late at night.

While the boys could never be anything other than privileged, she showed them another side of life and taught them to be compassionate towards others less fortunate.

Her influence on William covers nature and nurture. Tall, fair-headed and ever-so-slightly bashful, he is instinctively affectionate and at ease when meeting the public. He is very much his mother's son.

His desire to help others is demonstrated by his commitment to wide-ranging charity work and his career as an RAF search and rescue helicopter pilot, based in Anglesey, where he and Kate have set up home.

It was to William that Diana often turned when events in her life were overwhelming (she described him as her "soul mate"). When she was stripped of the 'Her Royal Highness' title in 1996 as the divorce from Charles was finalised, Wills consoled her by telling her that "mummy" was the only title that mattered.

Her legacy lives on.

THE NATION'S
DARLING

In a short space of time, Lady Diana Spencer rose from obscurity to become one of the most photographed women in the world. Her charm, style and unaffected manner won countless admirers

She's the best thing that's ever happened to us

THURSDAY, DECEMBER 24, 1981

By Marje Proops

It is difficult to believe it but this time last year Lady Diana Spencer was hardly more than just a strong rumour, although she was certainly the subject of a lot of speculation.

The gossip was that she and Prince Charles had been going steady for several weeks. But 18 months or so ago hardly anyone, apart from her family, friends and a few tiny tots in a nursery school at Pimlico, had heard of her.

Now she is our proudest national possession, the best thing that's happened to us in a year of misery. We've worried about jobs, about money, about inflation. Thatcherite gloom has clouded our lives.

Honeymoon: At Balmoral, August 1981

Our bills have got bigger while the pay packets (for those lucky enough to have them) have seemed to shrink each week. We weren't even consoled by a long, hot summer. We had a short, rather damp one.

But before we began to look forward to spring suddenly she appeared and the nation fell in love with the artless, modest 19-year-old girl Prince Charles presented to us.

I suppose he simply saw her as belonging exclusively to him, but he has to share his love with about 50 million citizens.

I'm told that dewy-eyed girls as well as their mums and grannies cut out newspaper and magazine pictures of her to keep in scrapbooks – any pop idol would envy her enormous fan following. ▶

It was on February 24 that Buckingham Palace announced the engagement and from the moment she appeared arm-in-arm with her fiancé, it seemed as if the whole country breathed a sigh of pure rapture.

Ignoring the disagreeable characters who will write to tell me I'm a sloppy, sentimental idiot, I nominate Princess Diana the Personality of the Year. Personality plus, in fact.

This has been a particularly testing year for such an inexperienced girl. But mostly she has stood up to it all superbly, and with enchanting style and remarkable aplomb.

To make the switch from comparative obscurity to almost overnight universal popularity and fame would have knocked a lesser young mortal for six. This shy-looking young woman has shown strength and guts, although she did shed a few nervous tears at one or two tricky moments.

She has made a few unfortunate errors of judgement — like taking a pot shot at defenceless animals and failing to discourage her Royal spouse's love of blood sports — but even while earning the disapproval of almost everyone for these lapses, she has been forgiven. We behave towards her like indulgent parents who forgive an errant child.

The wedding in July put us all into a state of euphoria from which we had barely recovered when the pregnancy was announced last month. We've suffered her morning sickness with her. We'll watch her anxiously as she grows more ample. We await the birth of her baby almost as eagerly as she does.

If ever a girl was the embodiment of a troubled nation's romantic, escapist dream, it's Diana, personality of this year — and, I suspect of many, many more years to come.

Stunning: In Brisbane, 1983. The image below is also from the same Australia tour

Woman in black: Meeting Pope John Paul II at the Vatican

Di takes it all in her stride

WEDNESDAY, JUNE 23, 1982   **By Marje Proops**

Di's done it again – giving us all yet another surprise. Amazing girl that she is, she skipped out of hospital last evening with her baby in what must be near record time. Just 21 hours after his birth.

She looked radiant and stunning, still wearing her favourite green-spotted maternity dress, plus pop socks. Prince Charles, though, looked a bit stunned. No wonder.

His wife, unlike every other wife I have come across, wasn't making the usual big production out of giving birth. So much for the myths and the mystery of childbirth perpetuated by generations of women.

Princess Di literally took it all in her young healthy stride. At the start of their journey home to Kensington Palace, Prince Charles was carrying the infant. He handed his son to mother before they got into the car.

Somehow, his mother had found time to get her hair fixed and her face beautifully made up. She looked as immaculate as she always does. Motherhood has simply added another dimension to her style.

But will other new mums thank the Princess for rushing out of hospital so swiftly? I reckon not. Almost all hospital maternity units decree a minimum of four days stay after the birth. And for most mothers it is a heaven sent chance to rest and keep their feet up as well as to have someone bring them their meals.

All too soon, they are on to the nappy-washing routine and the sheer drudgery that is the unromantic part of motherhood.

None of that will be troubling the serene Princess Di. She can comfortably nurse her baby, relaxed in the knowledge that somebody will get his daddy's tea and wash the baby's nappies. That's the bonus of being the mother of such a very important little baby.

A mother's touch: Holding William on the day of his Christening, August 1982

Number two: Leaving hospital after the birth of Prince Harry, September 1984

From shy teenager to a woman who stunned the world

MONDAY, APRIL 18, 1983   **By James Whitaker**

In the sun: Relaxing with the boys on holiday in Majorca

It was a moment to unnerve the bravest. There she was, standing in the doorway, taking a deep breath and composing herself to make her entrance. A thousand pairs of eyes were on her. They were checking her jewellery, analysing her make-up, her dress, her posture and even whether there was any nail-biting.

The Princess of Wales was officially attending a State reception in Brisbane. Happily, that particular night, Princess Diana, in a pink dress and wearing the family diamond tiara, looked sensational. It was possibly the most stunning she had looked during the whole of her month-long tour of Australia with Prince Charles.

As I stood and watched, it was hard not to think back to what had happened to her both physically and mentally in the two-and-a-half-years that I have seen her at the side of Prince Charles. The transition of Princess Diana from Earl's daughter to future Queen has not been done without a great deal of persistence.

The 'royalling' of Diana has taken help from professionals in many walks of life. She has maids, ladies-in-waiting, secretaries, bodyguards, nannies and a press secretary. For the tour of Australia and New Zealand, the Princess has taken with her two nannies, a cook, maid and even two hairdressers. However, she does her own make-up.

Diana has become almost completely 'regalised'. I say 'almost'. Knowing her, I don't believe she will ever become totally moulded. Her character is too strong and her determination too great for her to end up ever doing exactly as she is told.

But it is hard to remember that Diana, Princess of Wales, is the same person who, back in 1980, taught tiny tots in a kindergarten. Then she was sweet, as helpful as she dared to be, very self-conscious and deliciously naive.

But following the engagement on February 24, 1981, Diana started to change radically – even though she may not have realised it. She had to be shown royal tricks so she could cope with public engagements. The Queen Mother and Prince Charles were the leading coaches.

Most noticeably, her appearance started to change. Soon after the engagement, she still looked little more than a child.

Looking back at photographs of her then, she also appears to be almost chubby. She wasn't, of course. All she had was many more curves than she does now – and all in the right places.

In the two years between the photographs a great deal has changed. In fact, after comparing the photos, it is fairly hard to be sure they are of the same person. Note the Princess's angular look, particularly in her nose, following the birth of Prince William last June and a period of heavy dieting.

Observe too, the sort of jewellery she wears around her slender neck now, compared with the simple gold letter 'D' she always used to favour. There's more confidence in her public engagements as well. She will move from one VIP to the next, engaging them in conversation and often cracking clever little quips.

Prince Charles is largely responsible for this new-found confidence, but it is Diana herself who can take most of the credit. Only she could discipline herself to stop biting her fingernails.

Only she could have been so adamant that Prince William should travel with them on this tour. To me it is not surprising she is as strong as she is. She was always her own woman – and not a person to be trifled with.

For the last month the Princess has turned this tour into a triumphal march around Australia. Yet she still has the frailties that make her so delightfully vulnerable. She is terrible at making speeches – she gabbles through the words with no feeling – and she regularly gets more emotionally involved than protocol strictly approves of.

She will never be perfect at being a royal, thank goodness. But she has a magnetism that is the envy of every other member of the royal family, even the Queen!

Well done: Looking after William and Harry while watching polo matches in Windsor, 1987

Clockwise from top left: Reaching out to the crowds while touring Australia in 1988; Chatting with two Aussie lifeguards, also in '88; Sprinting for the line at William's school sports day; Charmed by a kiss from Luciano Pavarotti after a rain-sodden concert in Hyde Park; Holding on to her hat on a Far East tour, November 1989; In her element with a group of children at play at a Dr Barnardo's centre

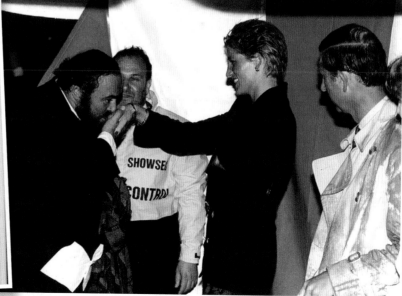

A Troubled
WOMAN

As the 1990s dawned, Diana was increasingly isolated as her marriage to Charles gradually fell apart, and she grew tired of incessant media attention

The rivals

WEDNESDAY, JULY 3, 1991

Prince Charles and Diana's 10-year marriage is in trouble – because they are rivals.

Yesterday, for the first time, a palace aide broke cover to spell out the reasons for the rift. The aide – a senior member of their personal staff – admitted: "The major problem is the rivalry that has built up between the Prince and the Princess over the years. They are no longer working together as a team in the way they once did. They spend too much of their energies in competition."

The breach of Palace secrecy came the day after Diana spent her 30th birthday apart from Charles. He had offered to host a celebration party – anywhere, anytime – with as many guests as she wanted.

But she preferred to stay at Kensington Palace with her six-year-old son, Prince Harry, who she called "the only man in my life tonight."

Heartbroken: Diana leaves Austria following the death of her father. In the top picture, she sits alone outside the Taj Mahal in 1992

Diana weeps for her dad

MONDAY, MARCH 30, 1992

Weeping Princess Diana was last night mourning the death of her father.

Earl Spencer died peacefully in a London hospital after a massive heart attack. The news was phoned to Di at her holiday hotel in Austria.

And as they began preparations to fly home this morning from their skiing break, Prince Charles was comforting his wife in her room.

The 68-year-old Earl was admitted to hospital with pneumonia nine days ago. Diana kissed him goodbye last week – and went off to Austria with her family, believing he was on the mend.

Then, just before 6pm yesterday, she received the shattering phone call from a royal aide.

No hiding place: In front of a wall of photographers after a charity lunch. Below, with Tom Cruise and Nicole Kidman at a film premiere. In the bottom picture, a young admirer passes a bouquet of flowers as she meets a crowd in Portsmouth

The broken spirit

TUESDAY, NOVEMBER 3, 1992

Staring bleakly straight ahead, next to her husband but alone in her misery, Princess Diana looked a broken spirit yesterday.

There was not a sign of the one-time 'fairytale' princess. In her place was a grim-faced wife and mother, forced to endure a marriage which isn't working – and sick of pretending it is.

Di and Prince Charles stood side by side at a cemetery wreath-laying ceremony on the first day of their four-day visit to South Korea. They were only inches apart. But for all the affection they displayed towards each other, it might have been miles.

The reasons for Di's inner torment became even clearer yesterday with astonishing suggestions that Prince Philip told her to "fit in or get out" – leaving her children behind.

A paperback version of author Andrew Morton's biography of the princess, 'Diana: Her True Story', tells of a bitter exchange of letters between the two royals. Furious Philip believed Diana approved the book by allowing friends and family to be interviewed. His letter, ordering her to "help maintain the dignity of the Crown", left Diana devastated.

Even Premier John Major tried to intervene in the royal wrangle. Mr Major is said to have warned Di he could not organise a respectable departure from public life if she persisted in "milking the media".

Diana ignored him and sent a forthright letter back to her father-in-law, stressing her role as mother to the heirs to the throne. The tone of her letter made it clear she was on the brink of leaving Charles.

Her new self-confidence paid off. Philip backed down and she was treated with more respect. She is quoted as telling a friend: "I wish I'd put my foot down years ago."

Morton has also been told Philip shouted at Di that the royals would be better off without her. It is said that Philip gave Di an ultimatum to fit in with the rest of the Royal family and behave, or go into exile.

Exile, and relief from a sham of a marriage, may be just what Diana wants at this lowest point in her life.

But not if she has to leave behind her beloved Wills and Harry. And that means, for better or worse, staying at the side of Charles.

Yesterday the world saw the result – and it was painful to watch.

She'll never be Queen

THURSDAY, DECEMBER 10, 1992

Princess Diana will almost certainly never become Queen, it was believed last night. Instead, her formal separation from Prince Charles was seen as the 'first phase' of a breakdown leading to eventual divorce.

Premier John Major said yesterday there was "no reason" why Di should not be crowned. He also said the couple have "no plans" to divorce.

But ministers said Major was "going through the motions". By using the phrase "no plans", he may have been deliberately signalling that there could be such plans in the future. It is a well-worn formula to rule nothing in or out.

Also, to insist on Diana becoming Queen when Charles is crowned King would be to condemn the couple to a life of celibacy. Now the option remains open that if the Queen lives as long as her mother, Prince William instead of Prince Charles could succeed to the throne.

The dramatic end to the couple's 11-year marriage came in a simultaneous announcement from the Palace and a statement by Major to the Commons. Under the "amicable" agreement the couple will lead separate lives but carry out a full programme of public duties.

Palace officials insisted that the split has no constitutional implications. Technically, Diana could still become Queen. And Charles would still be able to head the Church of England on taking the throne.

It was also stressed that despite reports of Diana's friendship with bachelor James Gilbey and Charles's friendship with Camilla Parker-Bowles, there was no third party involved.

The momentous decision to split was taken only in the last few weeks, Downing Street said last night. In the last few days Major held private discussions with both Charles and Diana. He is believed to have tried to persuade them to stay together, despite their mounting problems.

But they told him there was no hope for the marriage and it was in everyone's interest to separate. Charles and Diana wanted the news made public before their sons William, 10, and Harry, eight, returned from Ludgrove boarding school at the weekend. Both parents have spoken to the boys to explain why they can no longer live together. They will now do all they can to minimise the impact of their separation on the princes.

Last night the Queen and Prince Philip were said to be "saddened". But they are believed to be supportive of a decision which has brought a grim end to the Queen's "annus horribilis".

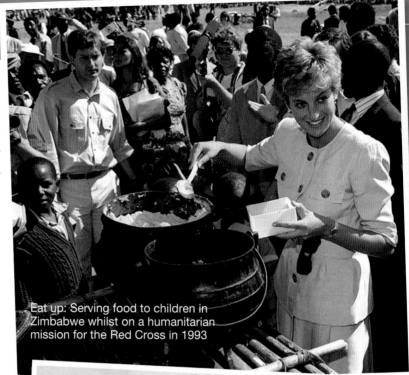

Eat up: Serving food to children in Zimbabwe whilst on a humanitarian mission for the Red Cross in 1993

Maternal: Affectionately patting a boy on the head while attending a youth theatre gala

GOING *Solo*

Following her separation from Charles, Diana began to relish her independence as she took control of her life

I loved James Hewitt

TUESDAY, NOVEMBER 21, 1995

Princess Diana last night sensationally revealed she was unfaithful with former Lifeguards officer James Hewitt.

In the most astonishing royal interview ever, Diana was asked if she had been unfaithful to Charles with Hewitt. She replied: "Yes, I adored him. Yes, I was in love with him." The 34-year-old Princess disclosed her love in an hour-long Panorama interview. Diana also told:

HOW she knew Charles was in love with Camilla Parker Bowles. "There were three of us in the marriage so it was a bit crowded," she said.

HOW Palace officials tried to write her off after her separation from Prince Charles as a "basket case".

HOW she believed she would never be Queen as the Establishment had written her off "as a non starter".

In a fierce fighting mood she said of herself: "She won't go quietly, that's the problem. I'll fight to the end, because I believe I have a role to fulfil and I have got two children to bring up."

Sign here: William writes his signature in the Entrance book on his first day at Eton

Revenge of the ice Queen

SATURDAY, JULY 13, 1996

Princess Diana was rolling in money after her divorce deal yesterday – but the icy Queen ensured she got little else.

Diana won a £15m clean break settlement. The price was to be stripped of her cherished HRH title after the Queen considered she had become too "greedy".

In another blow to Diana's ego, she can now do almost nothing without the monarch's permission. The Queen was appalled when the Princess appeared to leak details of the divorce talks.

Diana will now simply be known as Diana, Princess of Wales. Though regarded as a member of the Royal family, she will have to seek the Queen's permission to travel abroad on her charity work. And, humiliatingly, she will have to ask Charles's permission when he eventually becomes King.

Last night stunned Royal expert Harold Brooks-Baker said it was the first time the mother of a future monarch had lost the title.

Mr Brooks-Baker, publisher of Burke's Peerage, said: "It means

Diana will suffer the humiliation of being considered less important than all other members of the Royal family, including her own children. She is now a kind of sub-Royal – not royal and not private..."

After first telling the Queen she was willing to give up her title, Diana fought a desperate rearguard action to reverse the decision. She failed because the Queen and Prince Philip were "unimpressed" that she was originally happy to surrender a title personally given to her by the monarch.

The Royal couple were further enraged when Diana tried to win the title back by leaking information that the Queen wanted her to have it after all. Diana finally agreed to give up the title after asking Prince William: "Would you mind if I were not HRH?"

He replied with a smile: "I don't mind what you're called. You're mummy." That, Diana decided, was her most important title.

The decree nisi finally ending the couple's 15-year marriage will become absolute on August 28.

All in a Di's work

TUESDAY, JANUARY 14, 1997

Working girl Princess Diana got straight down to business yesterday on one of the grimmest missions ever carried out by a royal.

She landed in war-ravaged Angola to see the horrors caused by millions of landmines and told her startled hosts: "Let's get on with it." Her only concession to fashion was a Gucci shoulder bag bearing a Red Cross badge. After driving past bullet-pocked houses on the mine-cratered roads into Luanda, she changed into a white blouse and beige chinos, grabbed a large pad and peppered International Red Cross officials with questions.

Diana is here as a British Red Cross volunteer to see the Mutilados – the maimed men, women and children who have lost limbs in a country torn apart by war. The Princess made it clear she meant business as soon as she reached Luanda airport. She said: "By visiting Angola we shall gain an understanding of the plight of the victims of landmines, and how survivors are helped to recover from their injuries.

"It is my sincere hope that in the next few days we shall focus world attention on this vital, now largely-neglected issue. So let's get on." After a quick shower at the residence of British ambassador Roger Hart, she headed for the headquarters of the International Red Cross in Angola and began quizzing experts.

She asked: "Within the treatment (of mine victims) are you coping with psychological trauma?" Only low-level counselling was available, Di was told.

On running health centres and mine awareness training programmes, Diana asked: "How much financial backing do you require?" "More," was the answer. Diana watched, in silence, a video showing harrowing pictures of maimed mine victims and malnourished children caught up in the war. The Princess, more used to designer gowns, will put on body armour and walk a narrow corridor cleared through a minefield to publicise the plight of mine victims.

Shocking: Posing with landmine victims in Angola. In the picture above, she walks through a minefield, demonstrating the danger unexploded mines pose to natives in a country ravaged by a prolonged civil war

Di jumps for joy on her Harrods holiday

MONDAY, JULY 14, 1997

Princess Diana flung herself into holiday fun yesterday, determined to enjoy every moment of her stay with controversial Harrods boss Mohamed Al Fayed.

Diana, wearing a sexy swimsuit with match mini-sarong, jumped aboard a military style motor cruiser called Cujo at St Tropez on the French Riveria.

As the temperature soared to 90F, the speedy boat took Diana out to the £2m yacht Sakara, owned by the tycoon.

She was welcomed on to the yacht by Mr Al Fayed. The Princess then sailed away with sons William and Harry, Mr Al Fayed, his wife and their four children.

In the week that Camilla Parker Bowles had her 50th birthday, Diana sent out a message to the world that she is still a glamorous, young, single woman.

Thrilling: Having fun on the water with Harry in St Tropez. Below, she leaves fashion designer Gianni Versace's memorial service

Di's new man is Al Fayed's son

THURSDAY, AUGUST 7, 1997

Princess Diana has found love again — with the playboy son of Harrods boss Mohamed Al Fayed.

Diana, 36, returned to Britain yesterday after a secret holiday with Dodi, 41, on his father's yacht in Corsica.

The Princess shared a family break with the Al Fayeds last month. Then last Thursday, Diana flew out on his father's private jet for their idyllic six days at sea. He is a millionaire film-maker who has dated a string of beauties.

Year in the minefield

THURSDAY, AUGUST 28, 1997

A year ago today, she was alone — a Princess whose fairy tale had turned sour in spectacular style.

At 10.27am, exactly 12 months ago, Princess Diana's turbulent marriage to Prince Charles officially ended. At the age of 35 she was on her own. Still a royal, but suddenly isolated from the inner circle.

Her first night as a divorced woman was a solo appearance at the ballet, with nothing but a brave face for company. She looked nervous and vulnerable. She was free from an unhappy marriage, but the future as a divorcee was unknown territory.

But one year on, Diana is unrecognisable. She has put the past behind her and reinvented herself, even if it's not to everyone's liking.

Today she appears confident, assertive, relaxed and carefree. The starchy formal suits have given way to casual, almost glitzy glamour. The Princess is now a glamorous, jet-set girl about town with a new circle of friends and a millionaire boyfriend.

The gym-toned body and generous cleavage, once encased in sharp, formal suits, is now flaunted in low-cut evening gowns at night and shorts by day. The carefully-coiffed hair is now longer, softer and more natural. The long, lean body is, at 36, fuller, more curvaceous. At last she looks comfortable in her own skin.

But what is far more striking than Diana's new look is her whole outlook. Her words and actions send out the message that she's her own woman, and doesn't care what people think any more. Even so, the past year has been a minefield. She has courted controversy, had spectacular triumphs and scored some sensational own goals.

But she has never wavered from following her own course, even if it has meant flirting with danger and disapproval. Lounging in the arms of her new love Dodi Fayed or striding through Bosnia in designer jeans to meet landmine victims, she is doing it her way.

No one can question her determination to help others and maintain her pledge to be the queen of people's hearts, if not the nation. In March she met Nelson Mandela in Cape Town and offered to help him fight Aids in South Africa. In May she flew to Pakistan, to help raise £15million for Imran Khan's cancer charity.

And in June she strolled hand in hand with Mother Teresa through New York's toughest district, the Bronx. The same month, she raised more than £2million for charity by selling off 79 of her designer dresses at Christie's in New York.

But for every triumph there has been a near-miss. In an unprecedented move, she reportedly attacked the former Tory government as "absolutely hopeless" – something she's since denied.

And despite putting on a public show of togetherness with Charles for the sake of Princes William and Harry, she's let it be know just what she thinks of "The Firm".

There have been other gaffes, too. She issued an apology after taking the princes to a film sympathetic to the IRA. But it's her choice of men that has raised most eyebrows, and caused her more anguish.

As a newly-divorced woman, she despairingly told Cindy Crawford that she would never find a man to marry. She thought she might have found him in Pakistani heart surgeon Hasnat Khan. But in May, the romance fizzled out because he could not cope with the limelight or her "bizarre" behaviour, such as visiting his parents in Lahore.

Now the woman who once obsessively dodged cameras in a bid to keep her private life private seems to have found her match, and is almost brazen about it. She's been unfazed by cameramen as she has kissed and cavorted with Dodi. Her response to claims by model Kelly Fisher, that he broke their engagement, was to head off for a third sunshine holiday with the playboy millionaire.

Friends believe Diana has successfully negotiated the minefield of her first year as a divorced woman. No doubt, whatever happens in the next 12 months, she'll do it her way again.

On the run: Sprinting back to her car after leaving a gym in Earls Court. In the top picture, she comforts a distraught Bosnian woman whose soldier son was killed by a landmine

A Nation *in* MOURNING

Britain woke on the morning of August 31, 1997 to hear the shocking news of Diana's death, killed in a car crash alongside her new love, Dodi Fayed

Home to a stunned and tearful Britain

MONDAY, SEPTEMBER 1, 1997

Princess Diana came home last night – to tears, a dying sun and a cold breeze rippling the Royal Standard which draped her coffin. On her final journey from Paris, where she and new love Dodi Fayed were killed in a car crash early yesterday. She was accompanied by Prince Charles and her two sisters, Lady Jane Fellowes and Lady Sarah McCorquodale.

The BAe-146 jet carrying the coffin touched down at RAF Northholt, Middlesex, just before 7pm. The plane halted, the hearse began to move slowly forward, the 10 bearers began their solemn march. Charles was first to leave, followed by Diana's sisters. They took their places beside PM Tony Blair. Then the bearers did their work before the hearse drove off, led by seven police motorcycle outriders.

It was a terrible irony. Diana, 36, Dodi, 41, and their chauffeur all died when their Mercedes crashed at 100mph, being pursued by seven French paparazzi on motorcycles.

As the hearse slowly left, few held back their tears. Charles then joined a flight for Aberdeen so he could return to Balmoral to comfort his distraught sons William, 15, and Harry, 12. Their anguish was mirrored throughout Britain in extraordinary scenes as ordinary men and women paid tearful and emotional tribute to the People's Princess.

Charles had carried the burden alone as doctors vainly battled for two hours to save his ex-wife's life early yesterday. While his sons slept on at Balmoral unaware of the tragedy, he asked to be constantly updated. It was only after news of Diana's death at 3am came through that the Prince told the boys of their terrible loss.

Yesterday morning, as a disbelieving world paid tribute to one of the most deeply loved public figures of all time, the Prince and his sons attended a service at Crathie parish church. They were joined by the Queen, Prince Philip and the Queen Mother.

Charles then travelled to Paris, where he and Diana's sisters were met by French dignitaries. They were then driven to the De La Pitie Saltpetriere Hospital where Diana's body lay.

The first official statement confirming Diana's death had been released in the early hours. It said the Queen and Charles were "deeply shocked and distressed by this terrible news." The Government will effectively grind to a halt this week, with all policy announcements postponed.

The Mirror

Monday September 1 1997

30p

1961-1997

This was a day for trying to keep emotions under control. If the tears started to flow, when would they ever stop?

By Tony Parsons

MONDAY, SEPTEMBER 8, 1997

Being part of the congregation in Westminster Abbey was an experience that I will carry with me for the rest of my days.

From my seat behind the Spencer family, I had a clear view of Princes William and Harry. The boys carried themselves like men. Somewhere, their mother was watching, and was very proud.

Tall, handsome William, so like his beautiful mother, Little Harry, looking far younger than his years, both carrying themselves with a dignity that grown men would be hard pressed to match. Who could fail to be moved by the sight of the boys?

Some of the biggest names in the world were there – Tom Cruise, Henry Kissinger, Steven Spielberg, Thatcher, Pavarotti and George Michael. And for this one special day they were all just extras. Only Diana could have pulled a crowd like this.

There was only one true star in Westminster Abbey. And the sight of her coffin garlanded with white flowers made you realise, for the very first time, that you would never see her laughing face again. When the cortege arrived and you saw the faces of William and Harry behind their mother's coffin, not crying although their hearts were shredded with misery, you knew that this was a day for keeping emotion under control. If the tears started, when would they ever stop?

They looked so blond, so brave, so young, so dignified and so completely and totally bereft. Their world had fallen apart. Everyone must have felt like putting a comforting arm around their shoulders.

When Elton John sang of "our nation's golden child", I had to choke back the tears. And this was the point that Diana's children seemed to lose control. We had heard classical music, hymns, the golden voices of the Abbey's choir. But this was a song written just for their mother, and every line echoed with a sense of love and loss.

It felt like we all learned a lot during that hour in Westminster Abbey. The sight of those brave, beautiful boys showed us that there is a place for restraint as well as emotion. Elton John's emotional song showed us that keeping control and weeping bitter tears both have their place in life. And perhaps we also learned the depth of our sadness at losing Diana, our Princess.

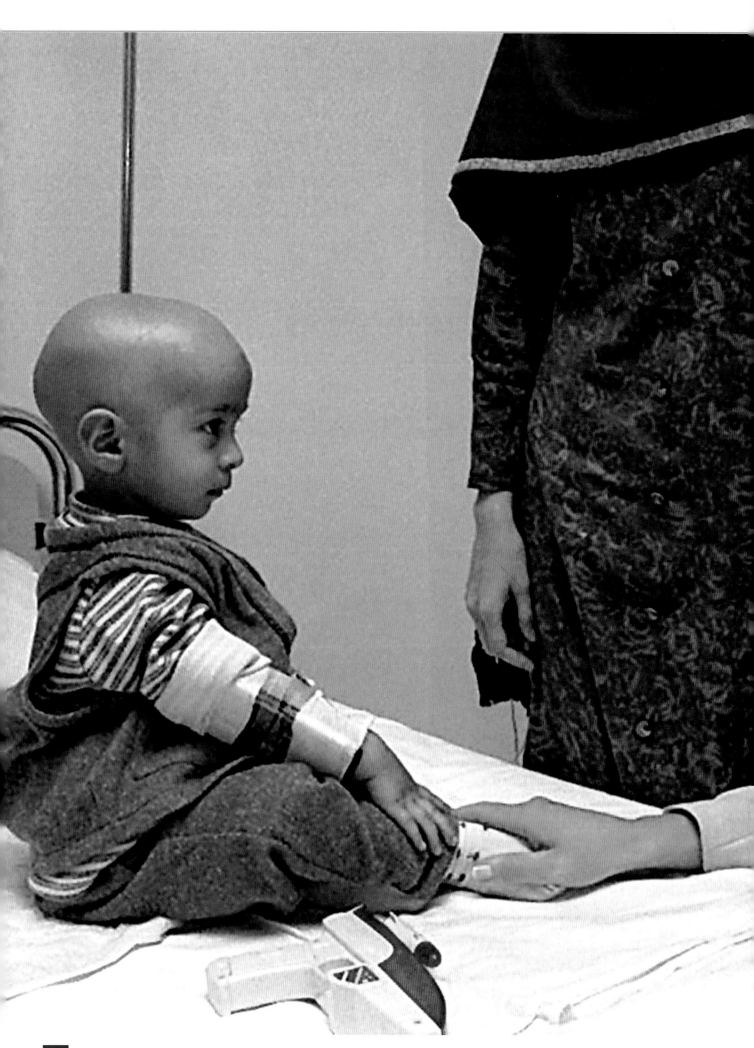

Caring: Reaching out to touch a young cancer patient during a visit to Imran Khan's hospital complex in Lahore, Pakistan, February 1996

WHAT NOW FOR THE
Fashion
QUEEN?

Post-wedding, the attention on the newly-titled Duchess of Cambridge has increased as every outfit and hairstyle is analysed and copied. The experience of Diana showed that life in the limelight can be tough but it appears that Kate will cope

By Victoria Murphy
Daily Mirror Royal Reporter

It has been almost two months since Kate said the vows that transformed her from plain Miss Middleton to the future Queen.

And, like Diana 30 years before her, she faces a steep learning curve. Now the Duchess of Cambridge, Kate is a fully-fledged member of the royal family, expected to observe all the pomp and pageantry of royal etiquette at all times.

When she was Prince William's girlfriend she could come and go as she pleased and her privacy was fiercely protected. Now, her every move is set to be lived out in the full public glare and she has already become one of the most photographed women in the world.

In her first few weeks as a royal bride Kate has already made dozens of appearances at official events and engagements.

She has met President Obama and wife Michelle, sat in the royal box for the Queen's official birthday parade, and is set for her first royal tour of Canada and California in just a few weeks.

Already every high-street outfit she wears is sold out within hours and her hairstyle is recreated in salons around the country. ▶

▶ With her tall, slender figure, emerging fashion icon status and a future King on her arm, it is hard not to see Kate as a 21st century Princess Diana.

But, in reality, the two women are very different.

Diana's fairytale royal marriage ended in a difficult and painful drawn-out separation, then divorce, and for many the warning signs were there from the start.

In their engagement interview on February 24 1981, Prince Charles's response when asked if the couple loved each other was unforgettable.

Diana said "Of course", but, in words that would later come back to haunt him, Charles replied: "Whatever 'love' means."

His response reflected the fact he and Lady Diana Spencer had only been dating for a few months, and shared very few of the same hobbies and interests.

They may have looked like the perfect royal couple, but life after the big white wedding loomed long and lonely for Diana when she realised she barely knew the man she married.

Their situation is a world away from Kate and William, who had already lived together for several years before he popped the question.

They share the same friends, enjoy lots of the same outdoor hobbies and, as a glowing William told the world when their engagement was announced, have a "good giggle" together.

Most importantly, they were firm friends before romance blossomed and William was determined to wait to propose so his bride would not feel overwhelmed by her introduction into royal life.

In his engagement interview, he spoke of "trying to learn from lessons of the past" and giving Kate the "chance to see in and back out if she needed to before it all got too much".

Making it clear he was mindful of the isolation his mother suffered, he said: "We've talked about it for a while, we've talked about this happening so Kate wasn't in the dark at all."

There may only be one generation between William and his parents, but the gulf between the marriage scenarios seems much, much wider.

At 29, Kate was almost a full 10 years older than Diana when she walked down the aisle to her prince on her wedding day.

Neither bride promised to "obey", but while Kate and William

Loving: Diana cared deeply about other people

Centre of attention: Charming a large crowd in Australia during a 1988 tour

In demand: Almost every high-street outfit Kate wears sells out within hours

had grown up together as equals, 20-year-old Diana seemed almost childlike next to 32-year-old Prince Charles.

But, despite her tender years, Diana's magical ability to captivate the public saw her effortlessly transcend boundaries of class, age, race and religion.

Right from the beginning of her public life she charmed everyone she met, and those lucky enough to be in her presence described her as "utterly absorbing".

A former nursery school teacher, her special bond and love of children saw her travel the world endlessly fighting for a better life for the poor and the needy.

She was the first royal to hug an Aids patient and famously walked through a live minefield to draw attention to the international campaign against landmines. "Di Mania" swept the world and she catapulted the royals into unprecedented star territory.

And it is in these large footsteps new royal bride Kate finds herself following.

Kate has herself described Diana as an "inspirational" woman to look up to, and told how she hopes to do a "good job" of the "nerve-wracking" task ahead.

But William more than anyone is insistent that there should be "no pressure" on Kate as she negotiates her own path into the history books.

He said: "It's about carving your own future. No one is trying to fill my mother's shoes, what she did is fantastic.

"It's about making your own future and your own destiny and Kate will do a very good job of that." ▶

Grand meeting:
Chatting with
the Obamas at
Buckingham Palace

Checkmate: Playing chess on a Far East tour in 1989

Her own woman: Kate appears blissfully happy

▶ And, while Charles was often left skulking in the shadows of Diana's star, Kate and William have sent a clear message to the world their future is as a "double act".

Their private secretary, Jamie Lowther-Pinkerton, has already told how they will be side by side for every leg of their North America royal tour and it is clear the palace is determined Kate will have time to ease herself into her public role.

She has also told she is "blissfully happy" playing the traditional role of housewife at their home in Anglesey as search and rescue pilot William carries out his military duties.

So far the signs point to a strong and united future for the Duke and Duchess of Cambridge, the royal family's brightest new hopes.

Soon the couple will move into William's childhood home of Kensington Palace, where he has many happy and some poignant memories of his time living there with his mother Diana.

Kate and William's new home is just a stone's throw from Diana's old apartments, and it is there they may choose to start their own little family.

Diana's boys, William and Harry, were her pride and joy and her greatest achievement.

It is a true tragedy that she never got to see the man William grew into or meet the woman he eventually chose to make his wife.

And as Kate begins to carve out her own royal future she can be sure that Diana's presence will never be too far away.

Whenever she glances at the engagement ring on her finger or into the eyes of her husband, there will be a little bit of Diana looking back.

William, along with millions around the world, will never forget his mum and the influence she had on so many people's lives.

But Kate is now set to write her own royal future, and only time will tell how that story will unfold.